ZEN EXPLORATIONS
IN REMOTEST NEW GUINEA

Adventures in the Jungles and
Mountains of Irian Jaya

Neville Shulman

TUTTLE PUBLISHING
BOSTON • RUTLAND, VERMONT • TOKYO

First U.S. paperback edition published in 1998 by Tuttle Publishing, an imprint of Periplus Editions (HK) Ltd., with editorial offices at 153 Milk Street, Boston, Massachusetts 02109.

Library of Congress Catalog Card Number 98-86918
ISBN: 0-8048-3187-4

Distributed by

North America
Charles E. Tuttle Co., Inc.
RR 1 Box 231-5
North Clarendon, VT 05759
Tel: (802) 773-8930
Tel: (800) 526-2778

Japan
Tuttle Shokai Ltd.
1-21-13, Seki
Tama-ku, Kawasaki-shi
Kanagawa-ken 214, Japan
Tel: (044) 833-0225
Fax: (044) 822-0413

Southeast Asia
Berkeley Books Pte. Ltd.
5 Little Road #08-01
Singapore 536983
Tel: (65) 280-3320
Fax: (65) 280-629

Canada
Raincoast books
8680 Cambie Street
Vancover, V6P 6M9
Tel: (604) 323-7100
Fax: (604) 323-2600

10 9 8 7 6 5 4 3 2 1   05 04 03 02 01 00 99 98

Printed in the United States of America

Zen Explorations In Remotest New Guinea is dedicated to:
Rob Hall, the leader of the expedition, who died on Everest
as he lived, helping others; all the peoples of the enchanted
African continent who should never forget to dream their dreams;
the peoples of exotic India where philosophy and progress must
always move hand in hand, and particularly to the one there who
helped to show me the way: Spirit and love on my enemies.

BY THE SAME AUTHOR

NON FICTION
Zen In The Art Of Climbing Mountains
On Top Of Africa

FICTION
Exit Of A Dragonfly

Contents

Foreword

Neville Shulman's book tells a thrilling story of his travels and exploits in Irian Jaya, one of the most inhospitable parts of the world, on the island of New Guinea, adjacent to Papua New Guinea. Irian Jaya is a wild and exotic place, full of lush and dangerous jungles, coupled with tough, rugged, sometimes razor-sharp, mountain ranges, with several of them snowcapped, even though being situated just a few degrees below the equator. Irian Jaya has been little explored, even to this present day, because of a number of factors, including internal and external political and economic conflicts, intensive mineral exploitation, its remoteness and inaccessibility, virulent malarial and other tropical diseases. Restrictions on access to this area have only in recent years been somewhat lifted, although unfortunately there have been some further internal conflicts which have again made it extremely difficult, if not impossible, to travel there freely at the present time. Neville Shulman is certainly most fortunate to have been able to experience at first hand its vibrant tropical beauty and to climb there the two highest mountains in Australasia, Carstensz Pyramid and Ngga Pulu.

As detailed in Neville Shulman's book, within the jungles and valleys live a variety of tribesmen, who are often dubbed stone-age because of lack of contact between the outside world and them over many centuries, even possibly thousands of years. The most famous of these tribesmen are the Danis and they are an extraordinarily friendly people and live a naked, open existence of which they are extremely proud. They can be very fierce on occasion, and there are times when it is apparent that the gulf between the way the Danis live and the way most others do is revealed to be immense and perhaps uncrossable. Possibly that is how it should be and I fervently hope that the Danis and the other tribespeople will be allowed to live in peace, unregulated and free.

Neville Shulman carries with him on this expedition, as on all his others, his own special brand of philosophy and it is this, as much as his fitness, which enable him to deal with the many dangers that he has to face in these very hostile climes. He always has fascinating stories to tell and report and this book is no exception. It will prove to be a great encouragement to all those who want to participate in similar adventures and particularly those who would wish to explore this wonderful place, full of mystery, exotic creatures and strange peoples, and is a great test of anyone's determination and endeavour. The book makes fascinating reading and will also act as an invaluable guide to anyone wanting to know more about and hopefully travel across the exciting terrains of Irian Jaya. Neville Shulman has a literary style that is lucid, enthralling and at the same time graceful. There are many uplifting moments and hopefully this book will encourage all its readers to learn more about this faraway, exciting region and its diverse culture and peoples.

Ray Mears

Foreword

This inspiring book tells the story of Neville Shulman's journey to the mountains of Irian Jaya in Indonesia, on the island of New Guinea - one of the remotest areas in the world. It is a remarkable story told by a man who thinks nothing of abandoning a hectic work schedule to undertake challenging and often dangerous adventures, always with a single goal in mind: to raise money for charity. This time it's for The Red Cross, for its work in Africa; and it's clear this adds an urgency to Neville Shulman's already unfaltering mental resolve to overcome any obstacles that might be placed in his path.

His choice this time offers many a challenge. Irian Jaya is an extraordinary and rare place, the interior of which remains virtually untouched by modern man. Few visit because of its remoteness, and because of continuing internal political conflict; and indeed, I consider myself very lucky to have been able to visit the place myself, to climb its highest peak, Carstensz Pyramid. The mountain was first climbed as recently as 1962, by Heinrich Harrer. It's a lovely, rugged peak; but it is the journey to the mountain, through dense jungle and over high swampland, accompanied by local tribespeople naked but for a penis gourd, or grass skirt, carrying loosely-woven sacks of sweet potatoes upon their backs, that I shall remember always.

As Neville Shulman details in this book, a number of indigenous tribes - often dubbed 'stone-age' because of their dress and their relatively simplistic way of life - live in the jungles and valleys of Irian Jaya. Until only a few decades ago, many of them practised cannibalism - and, fiercely proud people, they continue to resist Governmental efforts to change their ways.

This book offers a rare insight into the customs and rituals of these people. Journeying through their villages and invited into their homes, Neville Shulman paints a sympathetic picture of the colourful, eccentric characters he encounters. He describes his trek through the jungle and across that high swampland to Carstensz Pyramid and another of Irian Jaya's high peaks, Ngga Pulu.

On the mountains themselves - precipitous and snow-capped - he talks of mental resolve and determination and how, in his case, these attributes helped to overcome a self-confessed lack of climbing know-how. This perhaps is the most lasting message to be carried from this book: how, with the right attitude, you can do far more than you might think possible. This message, and the descriptions of Irian Jaya's jungle and its individualistic people, I will remember. Reading it, I wanted to jump on a plane and fly back there - if only it were so easy.

Rebecca Stephens MBE

Why New Guinea

The accounts of the greatest explorers hold a tremendous fascination for me. I have always been intrigued and inspired by the lives of men such as Marco Polo, Vasco Da Gama, Christopher Columbus, Abel Tasman, Richard Burton, John Speke, David Livingstone. Livingstone had also been 'lost' until that heroic journey to find him by the intrepid British-American journalist and explorer Henry Morton Stanley, himself passing into the folklore of the great travellers with his understated and almost zen-minimalistic words 'Doctor Livingstone I presume.' My book shelves are full of stories of their extraordinary exploits, courageous treks into the unknown, daring journeys to inaccessible jungles and faraway mountains. Perhaps Cesare Pavese summed it up well with his wonderfully optimistic approach, 'The only joy in the world is to begin'.

Africa is a continent rich with exploration stories and adventures, its diverse countries full of wonderful and amazing vistas of astounding scenic beauty. Although it has always been known as the dark continent, Africa has never experienced darker times than during this last decade or so, when so many of its countries and territories have been decimated by droughts and famines, as well as savagely scarred by massive inter-tribal wars and conflicts which have been fought without mercy to either side. By these natural and unnatural acts, hundreds of thousands and possibly millions of mainly innocent peoples have been devastated, maimed or slaughtered. Many brave charities and relief agencies have tried their utmost to halt this destruction and to repair some of the enormous damage done to the paper-thin fabric of so many exotic and special African communities; but they are indeed themselves fighting an uphill, extremely costly and probably losing battle. They need all our help and encouragement and I had been looking for a way of showing my own support for their valiant efforts.

There are some things in life you need to learn or to be taught, there are other things that happen for no apparent reason but which can have an impact on you beyond your wildest imaginings. You can always choose to be an onlooker, a spectator, a witness, when something momentous or dreadful is happening to others, about which it seems you can do little. Nevertheless, no matter how small the part you choose to play, it is always preferable to doing nothing. Your heart, your mind, perhaps your very soul, can also bleed with their pain, the torment some people are experiencing and you long to reach out and somehow help or at least let them know you care.

I had climbed and trekked in several parts of Africa, in that magnificent and beautiful continent, which somehow seems almost out of place, out of time, in this very last part of the twentieth century. Perhaps technology is just too powerful a tool, too much a modern magic, for the simplistic virtues of primarily agricultural countries which only want or need to move at their own gentle, unhurried pace. I have met so many wonderful Africans, full of humour, warmth and dignity, although they had little else, yet they deserved so much more and were now receiving so much less.

I was also feeling the stirrings within me to re-visit the mountains, to re-experience Nature at its rawest and most unexplored, to climb once again. It was perhaps a time when I felt the need to distance myself once more away from the trappings and the traps of our Western world, to shake off some of the bonds of civilization and to remember what it was like to feel not being totally in control and not knowing what the next day would bring. It is my way of journeying back to a time that all of us have experienced, when we had no idea what the future holds, what our individual destinies might be, not even remotely having a concept of how we would end up. Mostly we have all turned out so very differently from how we once imagined, guessed or even hoped we might. The refrain from a signature tune of an old television series kept coming into my mind, 'Whatever happened to you, whatever happened to me, what became of the people we used to be.' Of course luck and opportunity play such major parts in shaping our destinies but it is up to us what use we make of them.

Particularly I knew I was drawn to and wanted to help, in some small personal way, the peoples of the African country Rwanda. More importantly, perhaps influence others, either directly or indirectly, now or in the future, to stop and to think, hopefully encouraging them to give some support to the many Rwandans who are so desperately in need. The ferocious and deadly warrings between the Tutsi and the Hutu tribes that had taken place and were continuing in Rwanda were almost too painful to contemplate. Genocide had once more became a media word that was used daily until it had again become commonplace and had started to have the minor impact on most of us of our cornflakes and toothpaste. These terrible and base karmic influences were absolutely devastating the country. Apathy and ignorance were being allowed and even encouraged to flourish. We are all diminished by the hurt and pain others suffer; it is vital to realise and accept that everything in the Universe is connected, everything is osmosis. In all conflicts when any person seeks revenge, it is necessary to remember the old adage, 'First dig two graves.' That most devoted of relief charities, the Red Cross was working valiantly with the Rwandan people, as it does in so many other troubled areas of the world, so I decided my next expedition and mountain climbs would raise much needed monies for its vital work in Rwanda. Its refugees had poured into their neighbouring countries, Burundi and Tanzania particularly, but those countries, endeavouring to provide sanctuary of a sort, had their own considerable problems to deal with. The Indian philosopher, Krishnamurti, cared deeply for mankind and his books are a wonderful resource. In his, The First And Last Freedom, he states 'To transform the world we must begin with ourselves; and what is important in beginning with ourselves is our intention. The intention must be to understand ourselves and not to leave it to others to transform themselves. This is our responsibility, yours and mine, because, however small may be the world we live in, if we can bring about a radically different point of view in our daily existence, then perhaps we shall affect the world at large.'

Previously I had mountaineered in two African countries, Kenya and Tanzania and climbed their highest mountains, Mt. Kenya and Mt. Kilimanjaro in order to raise funds for some children's charities. This time I decided I should choose a more remote place, possibly on the other side of the world, but also with high mountains and use my journey there to fundraise for the Red Cross. Eventually I located the mountains I was looking for on the island of New Guinea, in the Indonesian part called Irian Jaya. They were the highest mountains in Australasia, both in excess of 4,800 metres, and I decided I would try to look for and join an early expedition to climb them. Indonesia is known as the land of dragons and fire and perhaps now I would find out why. Through my continuing interests in travel and mountains I had also come across the books of the Austrian adventurer and writer, Heinrich Harrer (once tutor to the present Dalai Lama) and learned that he was the first person to climb Carstensz Pyramid, the highest mountain in the Continent of Australasia. Carstensz Pyramid (Puncak Jaya) is just a few degrees from the equator line and located in Irian Jaya. Although discovered by the Dutch explorer Carstensz in 1623, Heinrich Harrer was the first person to climb to its summit and he only accomplished this in 1962.

Due to Indonesia taking control of Irian Jaya from the Dutch in 1963 and its Government's considerable concerns about security, it had imposed severe restrictions on access to Irian Jaya and its mountains and for many years refused permits and permission to visit the area. Therefore until fairly recently it had not been possible to climb in Irian Jaya and only lately had these controls been somewhat relaxed. Carstensz Pyramid is also one of the Seven Summits (the highest mountain on each continent) and those mountaineers who want to achieve the Seven Summits need to include a climbing expedition to this exquisite but inaccessible place. I had been working with Rebecca Stephens, the first British woman to reach the summit of Everest and we were planning for her also to become the first British woman to climb the Seven Summits and of course she needed to achieve Carstensz Pyramid. (In fact she was subsequently successful in this). Therefore I came to know more about this distant Indonesian territory and about the mountains of Irian Jaya and particularly the extreme logistical difficulties of reaching them. Apart from Carstensz Pyramid there is also another very interesting mountain close by, Ngga Pulu, a glacial mountain. Ngga Pulu had originally been the highest mountain on the island until the continuance of global warmings over many years had reduced it by some 20 metres, although that difference varied from year to year, depending upon snow falls and rock movements. Carstensz Pyramid is also snow-capped, but is mostly a very tough rock climb, whereas Ngga Pulu is mainly a steep glacial climb, particularly treacherous over the final ice and snow sections.

Through Harrer's writings and my own research I learned that on Irian Jaya, in and around The Baliem Valley, lived one of the strangest and most primitive tribes that still exists, the extraordinary Danis. This tribe, cut off from contact with the outside world over many centuries, were truly still deemed stone-age and they lived in jungles and lowland areas which were virtually unmapped and unexplored. It would also be a glorious opportunity and great adventure to meet the Danis, to observe their customs and the way they lived today, their lives so very little changed over many thousands of years.

I had climbed the two highest mountains in Africa, so perhaps now I could try to climb the two highest in Australasia. Of course that should not and would not be my primary reason. That must remain the need to seek donations to help the Red Cross in their important work and with their further fundraising. However there would undoubtedly also be the exhilaration of the expedition itself by which I hoped to achieve that objective. From now on, during the days I would make my plans and during my nights dream of travelling to the remote Irian Jaya region and meeting the incredible stone-age Danis.

The Incredible Danis

An original Dani legend tells of their belief that all people were born white and lived in a cave called Huwainmo. Those that emerged first and went to live in far-off countries remained white, whereas the Danis who stayed longer within the cave and their direct descendants then turned black.

The Danis still retain a very strong sense of their own cultural identity, despite the many attempts to change their beliefs and indoctrinate them into first the Christian and then the Moslem religions. They mostly live in and around the Baliem Valley in the centre of Irian Jaya and are divided into some thirty clans (sibs). The Danis believe that men and birds once lived together in absolute harmony, not realising that they were different from each other. As a result of this former relationship each of the thirty clans has developed an affinity with a particular species of birds, which are themselves then also considered to be clan members. The Dani men mostly walk around completely naked, apart from wearing a strange penis gourd which is held in place by one string at the base and one from the top tied around the stomach. The gourds are called either kotekas or horim and can be of extraordinary length, curved or straight and are invariably shaped depending upon the individual Dani's preference. Each man may own several horim to be worn on different and special occasions. He will often use the small open end to carry tobacco or money or even more bizarre objects. The Dani women are also more or less naked, apart from wearing brief fibre skirts made from grasses or tree bark or even yellow orchids. These skirts are called youngal and are short and slung very low on the hips. They are never removed, even at night, and it is considered bad luck if one is broken.

Conflicts within the clans mostly occur over ownership of pigs and jealousy over women, although occasionally over land rights and property matters. Their original warfare and battles though were often conducted in order to placate the many ghosts or spirits whom they consider sometimes live either within the villages or nearby. These ghosts are thought to control death and sickness and can cause illnesses to their pigs. Some of the ancestral ghosts were associated with vivid geographical features of the land, whereas others were related to the ancestors of tribesmen who had fallen recently in battle. These killings usually had to be avenged very quickly or their spirits would themselves cause great mischief. It has always been very necessary for the Danis to attempt to stay on the good side of the local spirits as they often make visits to their homes and villages. In previous real battles or subsequently in the mock ones, after anointing their hair, faces and bodies with pig grease, they always wear fancy headdresses made of cuscus, tree kangaroo fur and feathers of all kinds, necklaces and bibs of cowrie shells or pieces from the baler shells. Their spears can measure up to nearly 5 metres and they also often carry very long bows and a supply of deadly arrows.

In the past the women would watch the battles from a safe distance, bringing food and water whenever it seemed the men were ready to take a break from the actual fighting. A battle was always commenced by one Dani throwing insults at another. They were usually semi-humorous insults, perhaps highlighting the opponents' sexual inadequacies or other lack of physical attributes. The actual fighting lasted for only ten or fifteen minutes and initially there would be a sequence of small clashes, as many as twenty in total before each major battle, which itself would not last for too long. The warriors were always willing to postpone the action if it rained as they all especially hated to have their furs and feathers spoiled. They particularly very much enjoyed facing each other off in a kind of pretend conflict.

The Danis were never really very angry with each other, mainly using warfare as a kind of showing-off to another clan and before their womenfolk. The shafts of their arrows were always weakened about 10 centimetres back from the tip, to ensure the tip itself would break off within the victim and therefore cause most harm and pain. When someone was wounded his friends would then pick him up and carry him off the battlefield and leave him with the spectators. The death of one of them would not normally arise directly from being hit by an arrow, but from the infections caused through the broken arrow tip being dug out and the wound left open. When someone was finally killed and maybe a battle won, there would then follow two days of dancing and celebration. This was also another way of their calling forth the spirits of their ancestors to witness their success. Each defeat would trigger off a cycle of revenge, as the beaten enemy would try to even up the score by attacking at some time in the future. This might not happen for a week or a month or might only occur after several years had passed.

The faces of the Danis are strong-looking and expressive. They are more deeply-set than the Indonesian faces one sees in the lowlands, with many folds of muscle hardened across their faces. Their skins are very craggy and with lengthy ageing lines. Their facial expressions can change in a moment as they suddenly transform into smiles which seem to move in waves across their faces. When a newcomer turns up to join a group, all the others stand up and greet him with a cry of 'wa, wa, wa.' They like to touch him on the shoulder or the body and then will clear a space for him to sit down amongst them. If something amuses them or seems to be particularly interesting, apart from breaking out again with 'wa, wa, wa' they also flick their penis gourds with their fingernails. I was told this meant 'wow' and was a way of expressing their delight. Danis never wear shoes and their feet are huge and extremely wide, so very different to the ordinary Indonesian foot which is quite small. Some of them have calves like fissured boulders, which seem quite appropriate as they are often jumping from boulder to boulder with extraordinary ease. Their arms are so muscled they sometimes look like bundles of pythons tied up at one end, flailing around independently as their hands move. This makes the Danis excellent to use as expedition porters and to help carry the heavy equipment and stores across the plains and up the rocks and mountains. Their feet, bulging out at the sides, have presumably been genetically shaped from several thousand years of climbing sheer, razor-back rocks to which they cling limpet-like often at impossible angles, sometimes carrying enormously heavy loads. The Danis also have large, muscular stomachs and their buttocks are rather squat and broad - almost horse-like.

The pig is absolutely crucial to the Dani way of life. It is really the most important thing they possess. They can become so totally miserable at the loss of a pig, perhaps through his desertion, particularly if he was considered a favourite, that a man will often hack off parts of his own ears with a bamboo knife. Pigs are even treated equal to people. Sometimes the Dani men whisper into their ears like little children and they are often fed on bits of cooked food and allowed to sleep close to the fire at night. Like children, the pigs are considered to have souls, but obviously are unaware of any religious taboos they should observe and so can be forgiven for rooting in the spirit gardens or eating food forbidden to the owner's individual clan. However, in the way that human beings are just considered as part of the natural way of life and as death occurs naturally to them, pigs can still be killed, even in huge numbers when necessary, although this is only done on special occasions. In fact nothing important can occur without the slaughtering of a pig. Originally when war was to be waged the pigs were first consulted, then killed and offered to their ancestors in order to bring the warriors good luck. They are a major part of a bride's dowry and naturally a man cannot hope to get more than one wife unless he has a large number of pigs. The most senior village elders can get up to ten wives each if they have enough pigs.

Young boys cannot be initiated into manhood without eating lots of pork and first having a live, squealing piglet held in front of them to charm the bad spirits out of their chests. After the pig has been killed the boys must then go through a mock battle, at the same time experiencing the cold and hunger needed to make each one of them into a man. Funerals and burials of course also take place with the slaughter of pigs. It seems the spirit of the dead man is first appeased by being offered plenty of cooked meat, then it is driven out, before it can do any harm, by other tribesmen rushing through the compound hurling rocks, crying and shouting. The spirit then is forced to leave and must go and live in one of the Dani ghost houses. These are mysterious, square-shaped huts into which no foreigner is ever allowed to enter. They contain bundles of dried grasses, bound up to look somewhat like human beings. Often these ceremonies are celebrated all at once, so that marriages, initiations of young boys, remembrances of the dead, take place in a great pig feast held by a group of villages perhaps every four or five years. The pigs which have been so carefully tended over a number of years are nearly all killed and there follows three or four weeks of incredible gluttony, in which some Danis might eat several whole pigs each. The more you can eat the more favourable the ancestors will regard your village and the better it will be for a future marriage or perhaps a battle.

Roasted or steamed the sweet potato called hepere is probably ninety per cent of the Dani diet. There are more than 70 varieties of potato. The Danis also grow taro, yams, bananas, various greens, ginger, tobacco and cucumber. The gardens are very high-yielding and are sustained by a kind of strangely-sophisticated irrigation system that covers some twenty per cent of the area. The Dani women then scoop the rich mud from the bottoms of the ditches to fertilize the soil where the sweet potato vines grow. The Danis never live in large villages but form small scattered compounds near their gardens. Each compound usually contains some two to five families, who are bound together by a special relationship. Each rectangular compound is surrounded by a fence and at one end stands a domed men's hut to which the women are not allowed entry. Then there are several circular shaped women's huts which are just a scaled-down version of the men's huts. There is also on one side of the compound a long, rectangular cooking shed, sometimes also containing the pig stalls. The men and women always sleep separately and sexual relationships are controlled and limited. This is also to make certain that a mother does not become burdened with too many young children at the same time. The Dani mother is totally responsible for looking after the children. Men's work consists of the co-operative digging, maintenance of the irrigation system, setting up the fences and occasionally building huts and repairing them. Women work in the fields for long, tedious hours, as well as doing the planting, the weeding, looking after the pigs, the children and doing all the cooking. The only animals usually kept are dogs and the pigs. Only the pigs have the run of the land and are allowed to crash through any garden where it is unprotected by a strong fence.

There is a large, locally common spider, almost qualifying as a third domestic animal, which is encouraged to weave on prepared frames. The matted webbing spun by the spider is worked into fabric used for men's head and throat coverings. These throat coverings in narrow strips are considered magical and guard against the attack of evil spirits who usually attack at the throat. Most men and women carry string bags called noken which are made in a very loose knit, rather like long hair nets and can be filled with sweet potatoes, wood, even small children or piglets. The noken are knit from bark fibres that are rolled tightly on one side to be able to string. The colouring is made from various clays, orchid tubers and small ferns. Each noken is usually suspended down the back by a cord circling the forehead. Until some thirty years ago the only tools used were stone axes, scrapers made from stone or from boar's tusks, knives made from sharpened bamboo and wõŏden spears and digging sticks. Stones had to be carried from the bed of the Yalime River, which is about 150 kilometres north-west of the Baliem Valley in the Nogolo Basin. There are three kinds of stone taken from the Yalime River, the greenish andiba which is particularly hard, a bluish stone called wang-kobme and a black flint stone called ka-lu. Of course now the Danis can obtain steel axes in their trading, through their weekly markets or in the permanent one situated in the town of Wamena. Traditional Dani trading has always been through the bartered exchange of using seashells (the famous cowrie shells).

Most of the families, particularly those that have related wives live in communal type houses or huts. There is very little privacy and they see no reason why there should be. Invariably there is a central fireplace with it being the women's responsibility to make certain that the fire is kept burning. The women get up first and leave each morning, immediately after dawn, to work in the sweet potato fields or to look for firewood or to carry out any of the other chores that are necessary. The men take things much more leisurely. The huts are often full of roaches and the constantly burning fire is necessary to drive them away. Because of the proximity of living one with another, the Danis are extremely open about the physical side of their relationships, sex between male and female particularly. Even the young men are sometimes bonded together, this is known as Mbai, although only in the sense of being the closest of friends; perhaps a good way to describe this close relationship is that of being blood brothers. They often grow up together, work together, hunt together and even sometimes marry at the same time, so that they can set up a communal home. No one needs to be shy about the intimate relationships between any particular couple. If you come across a couple out in the jungle, even in the most intimate of positions, you do not need to hide yourself from them or not let them be aware that you have seen them. All you should do is jump right over them, yell at the top of your lungs and especially yell out your own name. If this occurs they are then meant to name their next baby after you. If they don't there is every chance the baby will sicken and die.

Another Dani tribal custom relates to the finding of a cassowary egg. It is essential not to pick it up initially; first you must run away, swatting at your ears and your head as if you are being chased by bees, Only then can you go back and pick up the egg to eat it. If you don't do this the egg will definitely be spoiled and uneatable. When someone dies the body is never buried but is allowed to slowly decompose, sometimes over weeks. It is continuously watched over, to prevent it being attacked by dogs or scavengers or other animals. However maggots are allowed to eat through it so that it becomes quite a revolting nest of maggots, but treated as occurring within the natural cycle of the life process, of which the tribesmen feel such a part. To our senses this may seem somewhat barbaric but the Danis are from a totally different world and this is their world. Skulls are always collected and stored, although they cannot be removed until they have separated on their own accord from the spinal chord. The Danis wait for the body to decompose and for it to fall apart, leaving only the skull as the final necessary part to retain. Eventually the clean, white skull is decorated, with even the eye sockets and nose holes being filled with beeswax and other substances. Sometimes they leave the skulls in certain places to ward off evil spirits or to frighten away their enemies or even as a sign of the way to follow. Occasionally the desiccated bodies of very important tribesmen (Big Men) are kept for supernatural purposes and it is possible to see their mummies housed separately within the village.

The Danis have many ancient songs, although it is rare to hear them sung nowadays, except in the privacy of their homes or the separate men's houses which are sometimes called Jeu. Invariably when they get together they love to smoke some strange kind of leaf or reed which has a very heavy and pungent smell. They also love to dance, but the men dance with each other, yelping and wriggling, each one laughing and jerking his hips in a way that shakes the penis gourd in the most extraordinary manner. Perspiration pours down their bodies and flies around the room, everything seems very disconnected and strangely shadowed in the flickering light from the inner fire. Mostly this is accompanied by incessant drumming. The songs are invariably of their past battle glories, of the times when headhunting was totally permissible and it was the way in which their enemies were finally defeated, so their heads could be displayed as trophies to the women and children of the village. The women are only allowed to enter the men's rooms when food is being served. They may not remain but after serving the food must retreat, so the men can continue with their dancing and antics which are hilarious to watch, full of fun, merriment and the very essence of the Dani way of life itself.

The Danis live their lives free of the constraints of modern society and follow ancient rituals and customs of honour and respect. They are not afraid and yet understand fear and truly understand, although without being aware of it, the Zen concept and the search to live without ego. At times we all yearn to escape, often not knowing from what, and in Irian Jaya perhaps there exists one of the answers. D.H. Lawrence wrote a poem he entitled Escape which starts, 'When we get out of the glass bottle of our ego and when we escape like the squirrels in the cage of our personality and get into the forest again, we shall shiver with cold and fright.' In the land of the Danis yesterday does not seem so far away.

Expedition Preparations

My search for background and more detailed knowledge started at the Indonesian Embassy in London. The staff there were courteous and considerate but had little available about Irian Jaya and particularly its mountains, apart from a few interesting but faded black and white photographs. This lack of useful information tended to emphasise how remote and unknown this area still was. However they kindly introduced me to the Indonesian Tourist Office. There an attractive manageress gave me the names of a few overseas organisations which might organise climbing expeditions in that region and I swiftly made contact by telephone and fax. I was quickly learning that the only reason anyone would be particularly interested in climbing in Irian was as part of their Seven Summits attempts and this meant that few expeditions were ever being organised.

After several fruitless calls eventually I made contact with a New Zealand organisation, Adventure Consultants, and as luck would have it they had an expedition planned for November later on that year and they had one vacancy. Naturally I jumped at the chance, overrode their cautious welcome and any of my own misgivings, as I felt all the signs were encouraging me forward and I was prepared to commit to the challenge. I did hesitate for a day when I was told however all the other climbers signed to the expedition were extremely experienced mountaineers, many of them in fact having climbed and achieved the summit of Everest. All of them of course would have considerable experience in the techniques of abseiling and jumaring, both of which it was emphasised would be necessary on Carstensz Pyramid. No other climbers were going from England and the other climbers on the team were from the United States, Australia, New Zealand and Japan. My resolve returned and I confirmed I understood and accepted the technical difficulties and dangers but explained how extremely keen I was to go with them. From my studies of Zen philosophy, I knew in accepting any challenge, whether a contest against an opponent, tackling any obstacle, climbing a mountain, three attributes are essential; technique or skill (wasa), strength or force (tai), spirit or mind (shin). The greatest of all these is

shin, as, if an individual has a greater shin, he or she can overcome
an opponent with greater wasa or tai, or even climb a difficult
and tough mountain which really needs specialised technical
knowledge and experience to do so. In sumo you will often see a
wrestler with greater shin overcome another wrestler who has
less. In following Zen it is said you require to carry with you at
all times three essentials, a great root of faith, a great ball of doubt
and wonder and a fierce tenacity of purpose. My enthusiasm
persuaded the expedition leader to accept my application; I
completed the medical forms, signed a personal disclaimer and I
was now a member of the expedition team.

All that was finally needed was for me to make my own travel
arrangements in order to reach Irian Jaya and then to prepare
everything I might need for the expedition. I soon learned that
another major and critical danger relating to this particular
expedition would be that in the lowlands and jungles through
which we would have to pass, before reaching the mountainous
regions, were probably the most dangerous malarial areas in the
world. The various strains of mosquitos in that area were so
virulent that the anti-malaria tablets that were presently available
would probably have little or no effect, and there was therefore
a considerable risk of catching malaria, which in this case could
be very serious or even prove fatal. I consulted my doctor Nigel
Southward and discussed my intentions and the medical situation
with him. He confirmed that the malarial dangers were very real
but was encouraging and thought I should still take two types of
tablets, two Paludrine daily and two Chloroquine weekly. There
was a much stronger anti-malarial drug on the market, Lariam,
but some people had suffered side effects and particularly when
climbing at high altitude it could induce dizziness. Dr. Southward
is a keen sailor and frequent traveller himself so he thought I
should definitely go on such an exciting and interesting expedition
and he totally supported my decision to participate. He explained
the best way to avoid contracting malaria was to avoid being
bitten by the mosquitos; therefore in the evenings I should always
wear long coverings over my arms, legs and ankles and avoid as
far as possible going out too much at dusk, as this is the time
when mosquitos are at their most aggressive and dangerous. He

also warned that mosquitos could also pass on dengue fever. He confirmed it was vital to take or boost a number of immunisations and these were to cover hepatitis A, tetanus, polio and typhoid. Fortunately I'd had most of them previously but I still needed several boosters.

I was told that some of the other expedition members were meeting up on Biak, one of the small outer islands on the way to Irian Jaya, in the main town also called Biak. Our flight out from Biak airport to Nabire on the main island, the starting-off point for the expedition, was scheduled to take place on a Sunday at 2.00PM. I contacted the airlines and several travel agents and learned that coming from the West there were only two possible flights into Biak to make that connection. One arrived two days earlier, some time on the Friday and the other 45 minutes before the 2.00PM take-off. Initially I saw no need to arrive too early and for a number of personal and commercial reasons I was anxious to save those two days at the beginning of the expedition. Additionally in case there were subsequent delays and I had to stay in Indonesia longer than planned it would be helpful to have days in hand. Also I thought it more likely I would suffer the possibility of mosquito bites and therefore be at greater risk of catching malaria the longer I remained in the lowlands in and around Biak. I presumed initially there would be little to do for those extra days, except become more anxious as I waited for the other team members to arrive and the expedition to begin. After receiving some assurances from the travel company I decided therefore to plan my journey out to Indonesia on the basis of taking the flight into Biak and arriving only 45 minutes before the take-off to Nabire. This seemed an acceptable proposal early on when planning everything but as the departure date drew nearer I realised that I was taking a huge risk. I was relying completely on scheduled transport and travel arrangements in areas where they had proved unreliable in the past and could be disrupted at any time. Soon I even started hearing stories about flights being delayed for several days, let alone several hours, and leaving only 45 minutes leeway for my final connection was obviously taking a considerable chance.

However I had committed to these flights and couldn't easily now change my arrangements and would have to continue on that basis. All I could do would be to take all necessary precautions and plan for other possibilities in case I missed the final flight out to Nabire. To maximise my chances and avoid baggage delays I therefore decided to travel only with hand luggage and that meant I must limit my baggage and could only take the absolute essentials with me. I contacted the expedition organisers in New Zealand and asked if I could hire from them any equipment I would need. This included the ropes, harnesses, an ice axe, crampons and a helmet. Initially they were surprised at my request and intentions but subsequently agreed to help out and would loan me whatever I needed. My greatest concern was regarding which boots I should take with me, as again to limit weight I only wanted to take one pair and intended to travel out wearing them. I decided to use Brasher boots (designed by the veteran athlete Chris Brasher) and understood they could be used for all activities, including trekking, rock and glacial climbing. The expedition leader hadn't heard of these kind of boots and although he advised that it was preferable to carry boots for all the different conditions we would meet, eventually he left it up to me. My need to economise on weight pushed me to taking and wearing just the one pair. Now of course, with the benefit of hindsight, I wouldn't recommend this approach to anyone contemplating this strenuous kind of combined trekking, rock and ice climbing expedition. Again the organisers stressed I should not rely on my flight connections going through according to schedule, that it would have to be my responsibility if I missed the Nabire flight and were unable to fly out with the other team members. This would then probably mean I'd also miss the following morning's early flight from Nabire onto Ilaga and might then never catch up with the expedition.

I planned my luggage and other personal items carefully, but no matter how I worked it they always seemed to add up to an overall much larger baggage than I could possibly hope to get through as just hand luggage. I kept trying to re-arrange and reduce the various items I would need to take with me, in order to cut down on size and weight but I still always ended up with far too much. Finally, though I would be travelling initially through very hot and humid Indonesian areas, I decided the only possible way would be to travel wearing my high mountain jacket and fill all the pockets with many of the hand luggage items, including two cameras, binoculars, head and hand torches and my books. The most essential and lightest item I would also be taking with me would be my Zen philosophy. Without it, my chances of reaching let alone climbing the mountains would be vastly reduced. As Zen Master Chao-Chou expressed it, 'Zen in your everyday thought.' I realised I must wear the heavily weighted-down jacket when passing through the baggage and security controls and then take it off once I had boarded the aircraft.

It was only a few days before I planned to set off that I received a communication from the expedition leader that there had to be a change in the overall logistics of the expedition. The helicopter company providing part of our air support had been advised that, due to some priority operational requirements (its mission work in supplying the local people with food and medical supplies), it would be unable to provide the helicopter at all the times needed. As they operated the only commercially available helicopter within 1000 kms he'd had no choice but to agree and re-arrange our schedule. He advised that one of the mountain guides and the expedition doctor would therefore set off a week earlier than the rest of the team, together with most of the local Dani porters and trek out with the group equipment and the drums and canisters of food. They planned to meet us at a place at the edge of the jungle, around 3,200 metres (10,500ft). The rest of us should be able to arrive there by a relay helicopter service around the same time they did. Once we had met up we would trek on together for several days until we reached our final base camp, close to Carstensz Pyramid. This trekking would also involve us in some additional scrambling and rock climbing. I realised that this unexpected news meant I really needed to take additional clothing and accessories with me, but as I was already overloaded there was no possibility of my doing this. In any case I didn't really want to take too much with me, because for me it was going to be as much an expedition of the mind as of the body. I needed to allow the space I expected to encounter to flow around me. As expressed so astutely, 'We shape clay into a pot but it is the emptiness within that holds whatever we want,' Tao Te Ching. With that to strengthen me I pushed the growing doubts right to the back of my mind.

Of course there was no direct flying route to Biak and therefore my itinerary had been worked out as London-Jakarta-Ujung Pandang-Biak. In case it proved helpful or necessary, the British Red Cross and the Indonesian Red Cross provided me with several authority letters which I could use to facilitate my travel arrangements and to ask for official help if needed. George Thomas, Viscount Tonypandy, a very good friend and supporter of this and all my previous fundraising efforts, gave me a personal letter which I could also use in any emergencies to help me overcome any difficulties which might arise. Additionally my private emergency plan, which I kept very much to myself, would be, on finding I had missed the flight to Nabire, to charter a small aircraft to fly directly there in order to catch up with the expedition team. Rebecca Stephens had told me the cost would not be high, around $400 and I would take this extra cash with me in case this became necessary. I was now, in all the circumstances, as ready as I would ever be and the date of my departure was fast approaching.

Journey To The Indonesian Archipelago

It was a cold and dry, late Autumn afternoon in early November when I set out for Heathrow Airport. On the ride in I carried with me the words of the passionate novelist, Ursula LeGuin, 'It is good to have an end to journey towards, but it is the journey that matters in the end'. I wondered what I myself would experience on this journey. Of course Homer, the greatest figure in ancient Greek literature, had stressed the vital importance of the same premise some three thousand years earlier, when creating his magical Odyssey, in making the statement, long before Zen (or even ch'an or dhyana) had been conceived, simply, 'The journey is everything'.

I checked in early at the airport terminal for my flight out to Jakarta, the capital of Indonesia. The aircraft was scheduled to leave at 6.25PM and was due to arrive at Jakarta the next evening at 5.15PM local time. The checking-in clerk eyed my over-extended back-pack rather suspiciously, obviously seriously considering whether it really counted as hand luggage, particularly as I was looking very over-dressed in wearing a mountain jacket loaded down with its vastly stuffed pockets. Before he could pronounce any judgement, I quickly produced my Red Cross authorization letters and launched into a somewhat complicated explanation of the reasons for my journey. Eventually he was satisfied and allowed me to pass through. Subsequently I boarded the nominated British Airways aircraft, a Boeing 747 and there was in fact plenty of room so I could easily stow my back-pack in the large, overhead locker. The flight to Jakarta was long but uneventful with only a short stopover in Kuala Lumpur to re-fuel. I spent most of the flight time reading and relaxing, preparing myself mentally for the strenuous times ahead. The aircraft arrived almost on time at 5.30PM.

After finally disembarking I made my way to the British Airways desk and contacted the staff there to see if they could confirm my ongoing flight and assist with my further travel arrangements. I was also hoping there might be some special facilities I could use at the airport that night to prevent my having to leave and check into a hotel. No one seemed to be aware of any so I asked if I could might see the B.A. General Manager. There wasn't one, certainly not one on duty that night, but fortunately I met up with Bruce Campbell, the B.A. Cargo Manager, explained to him the reasons for my travelling through Indonesia and asked for his help. He confirmed my flight out of Jakarta was scheduled to depart the next day at 5.00AM and he suggested I book into a hotel for the night and come back early the next morning. I told him I was hoping that there would be some airport room available to use, or at least a place in the airport where I could rest rather than checking into a hotel for a few hours. Campbell laughed at this and explained that the Jakarta airport was not comparable to the airports of major cities like New York or London, their own facilities were limited and the airport more or less closed down each evening until it re-opened early the following day. He also volunteered the somewhat alarming information that I should remember that Indonesia was really part of Asia and that it was essential not to judge it by or expect the Western approach to organised flight schedules. Although I was more or less starting out from its centre of the country, overall Indonesia from end to end is the same distance as London to Cairo and island hopping invariably would have its problems and possible delays. However he was very happy to allow me to use his own office in any way I wanted to, but this must also close that evening at 9.00PM and then there would be nowhere for me to stay. He suggested that either I book into one of the local transit hotels, until my take-off in the morning, or take a taxi down town and book into one of the larger hotels, possibly the Hilton. He was concerned that the transit hotels might be too seedy for me and might not be suitable, as they were certainly not of a high standard and might prove unacceptable. I told him I'd rather use a hotel close to the airport and therefore would be happy to try one of the transit hotels and would he recommend one. Very kindly he offered me the loan of his personal driver and car to take me to one and if it proved unsuitable he would then bring me back so I could take a taxi to one of the major hotels.

His driver did not speak much English and the drive took longer than I had expected. At one stage we were driving down unpaved, badly-lit streets and the surrounding buildings seemed very run-down. I was starting to regret I hadn't followed Campbell's suggestion to go to a more well-known hotel. Eventually, after losing his way several times, the driver asked some local traders for assistance and with beaming smiles they pointed out we were going in the wrong direction. After a further fifteen minutes or so he turned the car into a long, dimly-lit driveway, which led at the end to the courtyard of a small, wooden hotel building with some garish, flickering neon lights. They somewhat belatedly proclaimed its less than forthcoming existence and welcome. At the reception desk I asked for one of the best rooms and they said they had just one de-luxe room costing $49 per night. The hotel was listed as being two-star although it didn't seem to be worthy of any star rating; after I had inspected the room I certainly couldn't see how it possibly could be described as de-luxe, as it was dismal and basic in every way. However it did have a working shower and to me that was what was really needed. Additionally it had a telephone, perhaps that was why it was de-luxe, and eventually I managed to telephone through to London and spoke to my daughter Lauren, the only member of my family at home. I assured her everything was fine but I didn't know when I'd be able to call again.

The hotel coffee shop was open and I decided I'd risk the mosquitos buzzing around the courtyard, quickly darted out of my room, ran across the walkway and dashed inside the coffee shop to order something. There were also mosquitos in the coffee shop so I generously sprayed myself, the table and all around, hoping that would keep them away. I was the only customer and the hotel premises seemed generally deserted, but the meal was good and I was made to feel welcome. After several cups of coffee I made my way back as fast as possible to my room and quickly shut myself inside, hoping none of the mosquitos also got in through the doorway as I entered. I had brought a mosquito net with me, again in one of my jacket pockets and I fixed it to the wall and around the bed, by taking down a picture of an exotic temple and fastening the net to the protruding nail in the wall.

Previously I had booked an alarm wake-up call for 2.00AM but didn't think I could dare rely on that happening and therefore only lightly dozed, keeping myself more or less awake until my watch showed me it was time. It was lucky I did as the alarm call never occurred. I got up, shaved and showered, thinking that this might be the last time for many days and packed up again ready to leave. I had ordered a taxi to pick me up at 3.00AM and shortly before then went into the hotel lobby to check about it. I found two hotel staff stretched out, sleeping on sofas and woke them up. They told me the taxi had definitely been ordered and would be coming soon and I should go off in the mean time to have breakfast. It seemed a good suggestion and I ordered fried eggs, plenty of toast, marmalade and coffee. No taxi had yet showed but, after chasing the staff about it several times, eventually a transit van turned up and I was told this would be my taxi. The driver drove off extremely fast through the narrow, slowly awakening lanes and streets and we soon arrived at Merpati National Terminal, the time being around 3.30AM.

I now learned that the terminal building only opened at 4.00AM, so I sat and waited on one of the benches outside with a very motley group of itinerant travellers from all parts of the globe, including a number of Indonesians, several Australians and two German back-packers. Somehow the last two seemed the best bet so I asked the Germans how likely it was the flights would be on time and whether they were reliable. They informed me it was highly unlikely and on learning of my tight schedule smiled in great amusement to each other. They offered the obvious comment that I should have allowed myself greater flexibility in making my travel connections. They said they had become used to travelling slowly through Indonesia and Malaysia and most flights operated on a rather loose travel schedule and they always allowed extra time for cancellations or delays. It seems that even sometimes flights which are listed turn out to be non-existent. This was unwelcome news but there wasn't anything I could do about it now. After the terminal doors opened I checked through but found there were no direct flights to Biak so it was necessary to take the Merpati Nusantara 5.00AM flight to Ujung Pandang and catch a connecting flight there. At first I couldn't find this flight scheduled anywhere but, after considerable chasing around, eventually found it was being listed as going to Palu in

Central Sulawesi; Ujung Pandang is situated at the bottom of Southern Sulawesi and presumably the final destination was Palu. I also learned the flight was scheduled to arrive in Ujung Pandang at 8.20AM and from there I should then be catching a 9.30AM flight out to Biak and due to arrive at the scheduled 1.15PM. I enquired about the flight taking off from Biak to Nabire at 2.00PM and was told it was a normal commercial flight and was unlikely to wait if I were delayed en route.

The flight listed for Palu in fact left ten minutes late and I realised already I was getting behind with my extremely tight schedule. Once on board, after the usual take-off and safety procedures, I asked one of the stewardesses if I could speak to the pilot directly. At first she refused to arrange this but eventually, after various requests and explanations and producing my authority letters, the pilot agreed to see me. I was escorted to the cockpit where I outlined the purposes of my journey and my concerns of not arriving in Biak on time to catch the Nabire ongoing flight. I showed the pilot my Red Cross authority letters and told him about the fundraising I had organised in England. This didn't seem to impress him too much, so in desperation I showed him Bruce Campbell's B.A. business card and for some reason this had an immediate and useful effect. The pilot become suddenly quite sympathetic and receptive to my situation and said he wanted to be as helpful as possible. He agreed he would fly the aircraft a little faster in order to try to catch up the lost minutes. He also introduced me to one of his colleagues, Captain Rudolf Simatupang, who was also travelling to Biak and Captain Simatupang agreed to try and help me with any problems with my subsequent travel arrangements on the last leg of my flights.

Sulawesi itself is an immense rock island, but with forests and jungles throughout. The island is shaped like an exotic sea creature with its four main tentacles waving and stretching south and east, numerous small islands surrounding it and long ranges of mountains throughout, mostly crowding its population to the coastal lowlands. This island, like the whole of this region, is prone to earthquakes and when flying above and looking down at its rugged and inhospitable rocks it was easy to visualise the land moving in and out of control. We were soon flying rather low, zooming in over long, sandy beaches, crossing numerous inlets and coves, none of them showing any visible signs of habitation anywhere. Shortly afterwards we started to cross very dense, black forests, occasionally divided by curved, muddy-brown rivers, leading to huge swamp areas which often seemed to stretch right down to the open seas. The winds were fierce and the aircraft was being buffeted from all sides as the pilot started the descent.

When we arrived in Ujung Pandang in South Sulawesi, carrying my hand luggage I rushed through the check-in, picked up my boarding card for Biak and quickly passed through baggage control to take a seat in the waiting-room. After perhaps twenty minutes, to my absolute horror, on looking again at the flight board, I suddenly saw the flight time out to Biak was listed now as being delayed to 10.45AM, rather than leaving at the previously scheduled 9.30AM. This obviously meant I would definitely miss my 2.00PM connection, probably not meet up with the expedition members and therefore might not be able to meet up with them subsequently. I rushed back through baggage control and to the check-in desk and explained my predicament to the staff member there who fortunately remembered checking me through. I produced all my accreditation letters and asked for his help. He was immediately responsive, accepted the urgency of my situation and offered to help by switching me to another flight which was leaving in ten minutes time to the island of Ambon. This would only stop over there for a short while and would then fly directly on to Biak and should arrive at 2.40PM. Although it would obviously be still too late for my 2.00PM connection, at least this way I would be arriving closer to that time than at present and there was always the possibility that the Nabire flight might be delayed as well. I accepted this as I preferred to be active and it was certainly better than waiting around for the existing flight, which I anyhow guessed was likely to be further delayed. I followed his suggestion and he quickly changed over my ticket, gave me a new boarding card and I was rushed through baggage control again and just made the flight out to Ambon.

We headed out directly east over the mainland, across the Sea of Bone, flying over the mountainous regions of South-East

Sulawesi, again crossing numerous small islands and then out over the Molucca Sea. On board, not surprisingly, I found that Captain Simatupang had also switched to this flight and I asked him to speak to this flight pilot, in case again he could try to fly the plane a little faster and catch up some of the lost time. Simatupang promised he would but fell asleep immediately the flight took off and so I again asked to speak directly to the pilot. After the now expected delays I eventually was taken forward to the cockpit to meet this pilot, Captain Edy Sulaiman. I explained all the problems I'd had and asked if he could try to arrive at Ambon earlier and whether subsequently the onward flight could take off as soon as it was possible. Captain Sulaiman was very friendly and told me he was also piloting the second leg of the flight from Ambon through to Biak and therefore there was every possibility he could do this and move things forward. I gave him two of the authority letters I'd brought with me, which seemed to please him and he reiterated he would certainly try to arrive at Ambon earlier and see about leaving, if not earlier, at least exactly on time. I also asked him to contact the control tower at Biak and ask if they could alert the expedition members that I would be arriving late so they could be aware of this and might wait for me or ask for the flight to be held. The Indonesian Red Cross had also given me the name and telephone number of their local contact in Biak, Joen Diaz and I also asked if he could be telephoned so he could come to meet me at the airport and perhaps provide some assistance, particularly if the expedition team had indeed left before my arrival. Captain Sulaiman tried several times but could not get through to the Biak control tower, possibly because of prevailing high winds and suggested that when we landed at Ambon he would take me to its control office and I could try to make my calls from there. We were now flying out over North Banda Sea, across the top of Buru Island, before almost immediately reaching Ambon Island, finally crossing Ambon Bay and touching down at the Ambon airport which is situated on the Timor peninsula, a part of the island. (The actual Timor Islands themselves are much further south, down across the South Banda Basin).

I still had no luck on the ground with my calls and, although Sulaiman tried to assist me, we couldn't make telephone contact with either Biak control or Joen Diaz. However, as he had promised, the flight took off exactly on time and Captain Simatupang, now wide awake, went through to Sulaiman's cabin to see if radio contact ahead could be made. Our fight path out was over the tiny Haruku Island, across the large island of Seram (Ceram) where they have the Manusela National Park, to the Ceram Sea, before crossing Berau Bay, between the Doberai and Bomerai Peninsulas at the extreme Western edges of Irian Jaya. My heart was definitely beating much faster as we approached the final island, at least I was nearly at where my expedition journey should begin. Obviously I would be still missing the 2.00PM deadline and I didn't know what that might mean and whether perhaps my whole journey would have been in vain. I pushed those negative thoughts away and allowed my excitement to build as we came closer to the island of Biak. Then Captain Simatupang came back with great news. They had finally managed to make radio contact and he had spoken to the control tower regarding the 2.00PM flight out to Nabire. They had agreed to delay it and it would be held for me. I could hardly believe it and had to wait until we had finally arrived to accept I could rely on this tremendous stroke of good fortune. I hadn't really known whether the possibility of my chartering a small aircraft privately would have been practicable and I was delighted not to have to try and put this emergency plan into practice.

Our descent path took us across the Wainui Strait, between the Numfor and Num Islands, across the Aruri Strait, and we touched down without even a bump at Biak Airport. Captain Sulaiman had arranged I was to be allowed off first, and in preparation I had put on my mountain jacket and was holding my back-pack ready as the aircraft door was opened. I practically jumped down the steps and started to run across the tarmac. A blast of fiercely-hot air hit me and I felt the perspiration immediately seep through my shirt. I was totally over-dressed of course but there was no time to change or even remove the jacket. Everyone else was in short sleeves, mostly in shorts and the heat was intense. I ran into the checking-in section, a beaming, young

Indonesian called out my name and when I answered he immediately ushered me through to the lounge, where some of the other climbers were waiting to travel out. They were all in shorts and T-shirts and in my jacket and long trousers I looked totally incongruous by comparison. I was told most of the team had gone ahead the previous day and there were only now the 6 of us waiting for the 2.00PM flight. They told me to calm down, to relax and not to worry about being so late as the flight had been delayed. Somehow I didn't think it was a good idea to tell them I was the cause.

The Story Of Irian Jaya
And Its Extradordinary Riches

Irian Jaya together with the eastern half, Papua New Guinea, a totally independent country, is the second largest island in the world (Greenland being the first and not treating Australia as an island). It is also the tallest. A good part of it is covered with mountains with eleven peaks in excess of 4,500 metres. Although being situated a few degrees from the equator some of the mountain peaks are snow covered. The interior is mostly rain forest and jungle with huge areas covered by sago and mangrove swamps. The climate is always equatorial except in the highlands where temperatures at times can fall to freezing and even well below. The largest lake is Sentani and the capital city is Jayapura. At Jayapura General MacArthur assembled his fleet for the invasion of the Philippines during the second World War. Irian's 421,981 square kilometres constitute a huge 22% of Indonesia's total land area. The whole shape of New Guinea has been likened to that of the fabled cassowary bird and the westernmost peninsula, nearly cut off from the 'body' by Bintuni Bay, is called the Bird's Head - 'Kepala Burung' in Indonesian.

When the Portuguese discovered the island of New Guinea in 1526 they gave it the name Ilhas dos Papuas, translated as the Island of the Fuzzy-Hairs. It was a Spaniard, de Retes, who subsequently called it New Guinea, because the people there reminded him so much of the black-skinned natives of Guinea in Africa. At the end of the 19th century the island was divided between Dutch, German and British rule. After World War I Australia controlled both the British and the German territories and these eventually in 1975 became known as Papua New Guinea. All of Indonesia had once been a part of the vast Dutch Maritime Empire, the Dutch East Indies. When finally the rest of Indonesia received its independence from the Netherlands in 1950, the Dutch argued that Irian Jaya should be excluded and should still remain Dutch. They argued that the peoples of Irian Jaya were so different in character, type, outlook and physique that there was no link to the rest of Indonesia. Their religion, their lifestyle, their politics and history were entirely different. They tried to argue that Irian Jaya had no real connections to the other Indonesian Islands and was in fact situated on a different continent and was, with the rest of New Guinea, the northern edge of the Australasian Continent. There was even talk of trying to join the eastern part of the island, Papua New Guinea, with the then Dutch New Guinea (Irian Jaya) into one separate state of Melanesia, composed primarily of tribal peoples. The Dutch still retained control of the western half of New Guinea until 1963 when they were forced to hand the territory over to Indonesia, at which time President Sukarno named the territory Irian (probably being short for Ikutlah Republic Indonesia Anti-Nederland, ikutlah being Indonesian for join, although there is also a Biak word, irian, meaning tranquillity). Jaya is the Indonesian word meaning victorious or possibly good fortune and was incorporated to celebrate the taking back of the final part of their land from the Dutch. The total population is not completely known but is now estimated to be over 2,000,000. Within Irian Jaya there are a bewildering 250 different languages, of which the majority are barely known outside their own communities and only a very few have ever been studied by ethnographers. In Irian Jaya one-fifth of the world's languages are spoken there. The Western Danis, sometimes called Lanis, live in the highlands from the east of the Dani town of Ilaga to the edge of the Baliem Valley. The real Danis number about 100,000, although the Western Danis (Lanis) additionally total over 130,000. The cultural differences between the many different tribes are vast.

Although Irian Jaya's lowland swamps and coastal areas are extremely malarial, very uncomfortably hot and often impenetrable, they still have an abundance of natural foods, including sago palms, game birds, fish, turtles, crabs, prawns and shellfish. This is apart from the ever abundant sweet potato. Sago, laboriously collected from the sago palm, provides the starch that the Danis need and the necessary protein. Much of Irian Jaya remains impassable and has yet to be explored. The island's wildlife is possibly the most interesting in the world and yet the least known, visited or researched. There are over 2,500 species of orchid including the giant orchid Amophophallus and more than 16,000 species of plants including hundreds of species that are of medicinal importance. At least 124 genera of the flowering plants are found nowhere else and botanists suggest that further research may find 90% of all the flowering plant species here to be endemic. Some species are quite unusual. Pitcher plants have evolved a very interesting adaptation to nitrogen-poor soils. Their leaves form cups of enzyme-rich water which attract and drown insects, thus providing an important source of fertilizer. In the high scrublands, in the central cordillera, you can find the giant anthouse plant. This epiphyte grows outward from trees, looking like a large, very spiny pineapple. The bulbous base is honeycombed with passageways just teeming with ants. Even small frogs and lizards have been found to live inside this strange plant.

Mangroves and nipa palms ensnarl the brackish estuaries of the coast, particularly in Bintuni Bay, the South Coast, and the edge of Cenderawasih Bay. Further inland - in the Lake Plains region (Meervlakte) and in the south - swamp forests replace the mangroves. Irian's swamps harbour the most extensive collection of sago palms in the world. Further inland the swamps give way to lowland forest and forested foothills. Here there grows a variety of tropical evergreens with palms, ferns, rattan and many species of orchids. At 1,000 to 3,000 metres the forest changes. In areas with constant cloud cover you will see the eerie moss forest, in which all the trees are encrusted with lichens and mosses in long streamers. The pandamus also grows here producing huge fruits full of rich nuts. The farmers of the central highlands have exploited the fertile soil surrounding some of the river valleys, most famously the Baliem. In most of the lowlands with few exceptions the soils are impoverished and mostly barren. Past 3,000 metres, the forest thins out and gives way to strange, prehistoric-looking tree fern savannahs. Here also are sub-alpine scrublands of rhododendrons and stunted conifers. Beyond the tree line at about 3,900 metres you find sub-alpine and alpine heaths and swamps and finally above that just rock, snow and ice.

Irian Jaya is approximately half of the New Guinea Island and therefore many of its animals and plants have evolved totally in isolation and it hasn't been invaded by other species from Asia or other parts of the world. There aren't any monkeys or at least none have been seen but an animal has evolved that can climb trees and can live off their fruits and leaves. Incredibly this creature is a kangaroo. However this is the tree kangaroo somewhat different to the Australian kangaroo. Although it retains big feet and a long snout it has a winding, pink, prehensile tail and with this is able to lumber about through the treetops. About 650 different kinds of birds live on Irian Jaya and some 450 are totally native to the island. The Victoria crowned pigeon, the world's largest pigeon, is a brilliant lavender with a delicate crown of feathers and bright red eyes. Parrots, cockatoos, and lories brighten up the forests with their red, yellow, and purple colours. Irian is also home to some very strange birds as well. The megapods or brush turkeys, which bury their eggs in sand or piles of vegetation, are found here. There are nine species of bowerbirds, industrious creatures that decorate their large nests with bright objects such as flowers and berries, sometimes collecting small piles of objects of one single colour.

Pigs have only in fairly recent times been brought in by man and another creature has evolved that can roam about the forest floor and eat almost anything. Strangely the creature that has developed is not a mammal but a bird, the extraordinary cassowary. It is about 1.5 metres high, incapable of flight and very solidly built with a kick that can kill its opponent if it chooses to. These quite ugly creatures have powerful feet ending in very large claws, such dangerous weapons that they have disembowelled more than one human victim. These birds are unfortunately sought by hunters everywhere they are found and the hair-like feathers are used as common decoration.

All kinds of small creatures have also evolved, rats, mice, many of them more like the squirrel or the rabbit than the rodent, all of them marsupials but entirely independent from those in the rest of Asia or Europe. There are no other large predators in Irian Jaya, apart from crocodiles. Apart from man itself that is. There are also numerous varieties of parrot. Off the island, amongst the coral reefs, are many kinds of strange looking fish, giant clams, leatherback turtles and seacows. The inaccessibility of Irian Jaya, the intensity of the forest and vegetation, the inhospitality of the climate, have helped to preserve and protect this incredible eco-system of such immense and wild diversity. Only a few of these places are visited and allowed to be opened up and I was well aware how lucky I was. I hope the Indonesian Government realises what a great treasure it has here, will do everything it can to protect it and will not let it be exploited, as has happened so often in so many other parts of the world. The sparseness of the population that lives in Irian Jaya and its jungles very much helps to preserve this wonderful diversity, whereas in more densely populated parts of the world, as tribesmen have needed more and more food to support their expanding families and communities, so much has been taken, destroyed and lost.

Marsupials dominate the list of mammals indigenous to Irian. Unlike placental mammals, young marsupials complete their gestation in an external pouch. Wallabies and tree kangaroos, found in the lower mountain regions, are the largest of Irian's native, land-dwelling mammals. Other marsupials include bandicoots, possums and cuscus or phalangers; the latter are woolly, tree-dwelling creatures with prehensile tails. Unfortunately for the cuscus, its fur is as much appreciated for personal adornment as for its meat. Some cuscus are said to be so docile that capturing one requires nothing more than finding it and picking it up. Huge bats, called flying foxes because of their long snouts, roam the forests on 1.5 metre wings seeking fruit and an astonishing variety of these tiny insectivorous species fly the night skies. Perhaps the most unusual mammals in Irian are the spiny anteaters or echidnas which, along with the Australian duck-billed platypus, are the world's only monotremes, unique egg-laying mammals. When threatened the echidna uses its powerful front claws to dig into the ground, presenting a would-be predator with a back full of stout spines. In addition to this collection of oddities, most of the 100 species of its snakes are poisonous including all the 17 species of sea snakes. The death adder or the taipan are extremely venomous but fortunately are rarely encountered. The most beautiful snake found here - perhaps anywhere - is the green tree python, a harmless creature with strikingly green coloration and jewel-like markings.

The only amphibians native to the island are frogs, but there are more frogs than anywhere else, with well over 200 species, some hardy ones found up to 3,850 metres. There are over 150 species of lizards, some of the rarest and most pre-historic looking in the world. Although not a native of Irian Jaya, because of its uniqueness it is particularly worth mentioning the neighbouring Komodo dragon (living on Komodo Island) from the monitor lizard family, the world's largest living lizard and only found in Indonesia. The Komodo dragon can reach a total length of up to 3 metres (10ft) and a weight of 165kg (365lbs), is carnivorous and has even killed water buffalo weighing 450kg (1000lbs). Varanids or monitor lizards found in abundance on Irian Jaya are common scavengers and predators on small animals. The largest of them, the beautiful emerald tree monitor, may also reach 3 metres in length, although it is shy and not dangerous.

Irian's freshwater lakes and streams contain 158 species of rainbow fish. These small and often colourful fish are found only here and Australia and are favourites with aquarists. The Archer fish is a small, unremarkably-coloured inhabitant of some of Irian's lakes, slow rivers and swamps. This animal's special talent is the ability to spit a gob of water, with astounding accuracy, in order to strike and knock down insects. The insects are gobbled up as soon as they hit the surface of the water. Some of Irian's freshwater fish species are giants. The sawfish prowls the large river systems and some of Irian's lakes, including Lake Sentani. These distinctive creatures can reach 5.2 metres and weigh almost half a metric ton. The people living around Lake Sentani believe their ancestral spirits live in these sawfish and refuse to eat them. Zen master Torei stated 'Fish are in the midst of water, yet do not know the water is there, people are in the midst of sublime truth, but do not know the truth'. Water whether containing fish or not is full of life and movement and is an important element in the understanding and pursuit of Zen. The creation of a Zen garden nearly always involves the use of water or the imitation of the movement of water. It is often used in Zen koans, symbolism and imagery.

Lake Yamur, at the base of the Bird's Head, is said to be one of the very few places in the world where you encounter the freshwater sharks. The crocodile, now found less and less within the rivers and lakes of the Baliem Valley, is hated and hunted by all the different tribes inhabiting Irian Jaya. According to one of the ancient legends there was once a giant crocodile which crawled along the land trying to kill and eat all the people. When it was finally caught it was cut into tiny pieces and they were thrown in all directions. These pieces multiplied and turned into all those who then lived in foreign countries. There is always great rejoicing amongst the tribes whenever a crocodile is killed.

The colourful princes of Irian's insect fauna are the birdwing butterflies. They are quite extraordinary in shape and size and I understand that some can span 30 centimetres across. They can be found in all parts but reach their greatest numbers and diversity in the Arfak Mountains just inland from Manokwari. These butterflies are often covered with shimmering colours. There are probably almost 100,000 insect species and many of these are still waiting to be catalogued. In the forests you can find giant stick insects and katydids - some of them startlingly accurate mimics of their surroundings. There are tens of thousands of species of beetles. The capricorn beetle, a tank of a creature, lays its eggs on the sago palm and its large larvae are prized as food. The sago grubs are an essential feature of every ceremonial banquet. Spiders too are found here in great numbers - some 800 species. These include the formidable giant bird-eating spider, whose size and aggressiveness causes it to be rightly feared.

Irian has the world's second-largest rainforest (after the Amazon) and has the largest tracts of undisturbed lowland rainforest in all of South East Asia. These lowland, alluvial forests contain valuable timber reserves, making them a major target of the ever-growing logging industry. However, almost 20% of the province's land area is a conservation area of one kind or another, making Irian Jaya - at least on paper - one of the best-protected areas in the world. There is an important glorious proverb always to remember, although its origins are lost in antiquity. 'Those who plant trees love others besides themselves'. Anyone who for whatever reason cuts one tree down should be forced to plant two in its place. Otherwise, if the present rate of destruction is allowed to continue, in less than half a century there will be virtually no rain forests left in the world for those that come after us to enjoy. As the Inuits (Eskimos) state, 'We all inherit the world from our children'. Although the problems of exploitation are still great, Irian's inherent ruggedness and isolation do a lot to insure the protection of its forests. Also, unlike Borneo, Irian is not very rich in the most valuable species of tropical hardwoods. Irian Jaya has paradoxically possibly only survived through its isolation. In other parts of Indonesia, like Java, as in much of South East Asia, the soils are deep, black and volcanic, certainly some of the best soils in the world. In Irian Jaya they are mostly the opposite. Therefore the land can only support a very small population; intensive farming would destroy the land totally within a few decades, as the top soil is just too thin to re-fertilise itself automatically. At first glance it seems that there is plenty of empty land but in fact the land is fully utilised as it can only cope with the small number of people that actually live off it.

Not only are the forests of Irian Jaya under threat but many of the exotic birds and animals, the parrots and cockatoos, the crocodiles, are now being hunted, captured and sold and the numbers of all these extraordinary creatures are being decimated, without thought for the future generations who might never see them. Crocodile skins are being made into shoes and handbags, the birds of paradise are being stuffed for display, the best reefs in the world are being dynamited by fishermen, the shells of the giant clams broken up to make terrazzo floors, seacows killed for their teeth (often made into cigarette holders), turtles are caught as they come up the beaches and sold as varnished souvenirs. You can understand why the Danis and other tribes people sometime retaliate harshly against those who intrude, take and only leave devastation and destruction behind.

The Baliem Valley, 1,580 metres (5,200 feet) above sea level, 37 miles long and 10 miles wide, was only discovered in 1938 by the explorer Richard Archbold, as he was flying a small plane named the Guba over the crest of the central highlands of New Guinea. The mountains were jagged and barren, barely able to support more than a few tiny villages around which the tribesmen were carrying out some form of primitive farming. He could see the snow on some of the mountain peaks break through the strings of cloud, peaking out yellow and grey-white at over 4,300 metres (14,000 feet). Suddenly the high ground fell away and Archbold found that he was heading over a valley set beneath immense, sheer rock walls. He had inadvertently discovered the very last primitive civilisation on earth. Sheltered in the approximately 10 mile plain between the mountains was a flat, green land, intricately cultivated with clusters of small round and rectangular huts, mostly thatched. Round them wound irrigation ditches like spiral mazes with heaped up greenery in between. He saw naked, black figures running to hide and that was his first sightings of the Danis. The people Archbold had found had lived independently of the rest of the outside world for possibly 10,000 years. They had not felt the influence of any modern technology and everything they had developed had evolved only through their own primary knowledge and background. Archbold had uncovered a stone-age culture which had been totally hidden from the rest of the world. Even now some sixty years later it is still basically the same.

Fortunately in many ways, because of the strict security regulations that have governed this area for most of the time since it had been discovered, first controlled by the Dutch and then by the Indonesian government, it has been extremely difficult to obtain permits to travel through Irian Jaya. Foreigners and even other Indonesian visitors were viewed with considerable suspicion. This meant that the rate of progress and change has been extremely slow and therefore it is not difficult to imagine what it had been like over the past centuries. The immense distances to be travelled through it and the very tough and difficult terrains of these territories are also reasons why this area has been so unexplored until very recent times. There is still so much yet to be discovered and the very hostile environment, the harsh mountains and virulent malarial mosquitos mean that only very dedicated travellers or mountaineers with a particular purpose are prepared to journey here.

Irian's mountains are geologically very recent, consisting mostly of sedimentary limestones, sandstones and shale that have been uplifted and faulted on a massive scale by plate movements. The central cordillera tracks the exact line where the Sahul Shelf and the Pacific Ocean Plate connect. Volcanic rock is rather rare in the mountains, but in one of the few places where an igneous intrusion is found - in the Sudirman Range - the outcrop has proved to be extremely rich in copper, gold and silver. The central mountain chain comprises three connecting ranges; the Wisnumurti Range, running westward from the Papua New Guinea border; the Jayawijaya Range, bordering the southern end of the Baliem Valley; the Sudirman Range, reaching west to the Paniai Lakes. The Wisnumurtis are topped by Gunung Mandala (formerly Mt. Juliana) at 4,700 metres and Puncak Yamin at 4,595 metres. Gunung Trikora (formerly Mt. Wilhelmina) crowns the Jayawijaya Range just southwest of the Baliem Valley, reaching 4,743 metres. Irian's highest peak is the glory of the Sudirman Range: Puncak Jayakesuma (Carstensz Pyramid) or simply Puncak Jaya. Reaching 4,884 metres this is the highest point between the Himalayas and the Andes. Several other peaks in the area top 4,000 metres, including Ngga Pulu (4,865 metres). Although Ngga Pulu had been the highest peak previously, global warming has reduced it by some 20 metres to make it slightly shorter. Some still argue that at times it can still be higher, depending on snowfalls, rock movements and the weather conditions. The south-facing slopes of the mountain chain fall off sharply, yielding to dense forest and then coastal swamps. In the west - near the island's 'neck' - these slopes are steep ridges of sedimentary rock, scarred by landslides and cut by short, powerful rivers which spill from great gorges just a few kilometres from the coast. East of Puncak Jaya the southern coastal forest broadens and the swamplands around the Casuarina Coast are vast, reaching 300 kilometres inland. Several rivers here are navigable almost to the mountains and the land is so flat that tides affect river height far inland. At the far South Eastern corner of Irian Jaya, near Merauke, there is an extensive irregular area of dry, grassy savannah. Its environment, which seems to be more like that of Australia or Africa, supports great numbers of deer and wallabies.

The northern slopes of the mountains around the Lake Plains region, or Meervlakte are flat and swampy, full of nipa palms and lowland forest and little explored. The Mamberamo and its two main tributaries - Thearitatu (formerly Idenburgh) flowing from the east and the Tariku (formerly Rouffaer) from the west - are slow, silty meandering rivers. Thousands of oxbow lakes and other shallow, sometimes seasonal lakes dot the region.

Bintuni Bay cuts deep into Irian, and its inner reaches form one of the most extensive mangrove swamps in the world. North of Bintuni is the Bird's Head, which is made up of lowland forest to the south and more mountainous regions to the north, marked by the Tamrau Mountains and the Arfak Mountains near Manokwari. Parts of the Bird's Head exhibit karst formations, the tropical climate having weathered the limestones to fantastically shaped spires and gorges. The many islands around Irian Jaya include Yos Sudarso Island (also called Kimaam), 170 by 100 kilometres, but low and swampy and separated from the mainland only by a narrow channel. Off the Bird's Head are the Raja Empat islands; Waigeo, the largest; Batanta and Salawati; Misool which takes its name from a medicinal bark prized by the Javanese. Cenderawasih (Bird of Paradise) Bay (formerly Geelvink), contains numerous small islands and to its north are the larger islands of Biak, Supiori, Numfor and Yapen.

The peoples of Indonesia are the fifth most numerous on earth, with numerous and extraordinarily diverse cultures. Irian Jaya is the most eastern part of the Indonesian territory whose Dani people still use their original stone tools, unless they have traded them in for metal ones. They still fight with wooden-headed arrows and are fiercely protective of their lands and contest any intrusion by their neighbours from the adjoining valleys. In the southern swamps, the world's largest and least penetrable of all, there is probably still headhunting and cannibalism, although officially it does not exist. This is probably the last place on earth where unknown tribes are still likely to exist. In the past the tribal peoples have tried to oppose being ruled from Jakarta, believing they were entitled to their own way of life and they should be treated as a separate country. They believed their lands had been taken over unfairly, without their consent, by the government of Indonesia. At one time they even backed up these claims by trying to fight the army sent from Jakarta with poisoned arrows and wooden spears, but of course they had no chance against the military might sent to impose order. Although Indonesia is primarily a Moslem country, its peoples are however very tolerant towards other religions. During the Dutch occupation of Indonesia a number of churches were built and there is still a large Christian minority. In many Indonesian villages it is quite common to see the mosque and the church side by side, even sometimes sharing gardens. Irian Jaya probably has a larger Protestant population than any other Indonesian region, arising through the extensive work of the missionaries, but again there is complete religious tolerance.

Within the whole of the Indonesian archipelago there are only two groups that have really felt that they should not be governed and controlled from Jakarta and by the Indonesian Government, those living in East Timor and those in Irian Jaya. Both territories have organised rebel groups from time to time, but only the East Timor people seems to be taking it really seriously and have been extremely aggressive and vigorous in their response and opposition. However even in Irian Jaya, exactly where I had been travelling, a year after our expedition, some rebels based in the jungle took hostages in order to obtain publicity for their case for official separation. Because of these continuing internal problems, there have been further considerable restrictions on travelling to either area and for Irian Jaya numerous permits are required, which need to be very specific about the reasons why people are travelling there and what they would do once they arrive. After the opening up of the Carstensz Pyramid and Ngga Pulu mountain areas it is obviously a legitimate reason to travel to Irian Jaya to climb these mountains, but anything else is looked upon with some suspicion. Further down the Carstensz Valley the mining complex based at Freeport is usually totally out of bounds and there are all kinds of problems that occur if anyone strays off their agreed route near there. Out of all our party I was the only one who had any particular desire to visit the Freeport Mines; I had been given an introduction to the General Manager and hoped there'd be an opportunity to arrange a visit.

Despite the extreme friendliness of the Indonesian people themselves, it should always be remembered that the whole country is organised more in the form of a police state and is very much under the control of the armed forces. If there are any suspicions about their intentions then travellers would usually be arrested, and may even be held in prison until their credentials have been checked.

Travelling To The Heartland, Nabire And Ilaga

Our Indonesian mountain guide, Ripto, very young looking, ever smiling, had arrived at Biak airport to take us through to the town of Nabire and if he knew I was the cause of the aircraft's delay he never let on. Eventually we all flew out at about 3.30PM, urgently scrambling on board the two-engine thirty-seater Twin Otter. All our back-packs were quickly bundled haphazardly at the rear of the aircraft and we strapped ourselves in the front seats, very close to the open cockpit. All the remaining seats were taken by Indonesian soldiers which seemed a little ominous. There were no safety instructions given but there were two pilots and they seemed well in control. In our seat pockets we found small food packs containing sandwiches and a bottle of water and we munched excitedly as the aircraft took off in a steep, almost vertical climb before settling into its flight path.

We flew directly south across the Yapen Strait, crossing the island of Yapen itself, then across the smaller Ambai islands, before continuing directly south across the open sea, the mainland on our left to the east and then heading into the Cenderawasih Bay. In about one hour we reached Nabire on the mainland coast, just before the beginning of the Kobowre mountains. To the east and south Nabire is surrounded by mountain ranges, to the north-east the Van Rees, to the south-west the Wondiwoi and across the Kobowre, the Sudirman range where awaiting us were Carstensz Pyramid and Ngga Pulu. I felt I had really arrived now in Irian Jaya. What wonders would I find. I was absolutely excited by the unknown awaiting me in the hours and days that lay ahead. Perhaps the poet William Blake has summed it up as eloquently as anyone, 'To see a World in the grain of sand and a Heaven in a wild flower, hold infinity in the palm of your hand and eternity in an hour'.

Ripto was in charge of arranging all the permits and there seemed to be no problems and he proved to be an excellent organiser. He was also a first class mountaineer and had climbed Carstensz Pyramid and many other mountains in the region. He and I walked together from the airport to the Nabire hotel some 800 metres further on, and he was always happy to stop and respond to my many questions about the life of those living around here. I was sharing a room with an American climber, Tom Williams and after we had both unpacked I fixed up my mosquito net. Williams however told me he and the others were not bothering with mosquito nets or even taking malaria tablets, and they were prepared to leave these matters to chance. He doubted we'd be here long enough to run any real risk. It made me feel a bit self conscious about the mosquito net draped over the bed, but having carried it all this way I was determined to use it. The weather was very hot, humid and it felt very sticky, so as soon as we were ready we all congregated in the dining room to buy lots of bottled water and beer. I met most of the other climbers and explained the tight travelling itinerary I had followed to get here. All the same they were somewhat taken aback at my lack of equipment and accessories, particularly as they seemed loaded down with all the latest equipment, harnesses, helmets and boots. They couldn't quite believe I'd travelled here in the same pair of boots I intended to use for everything and in all conditions.

Quite suddenly the regular afternoon monsoon arrived and the rain poured down as if it would never stop. Monsoon is an arabic word meaning 'a season of wind', and the monsoon season occurs when very hot air constantly rises and causes the clouds to ferment and the heaviest rainfalls then occur. Its tremendous, almost overpowering force could be measured by the way the rain water rebounded upwards from the ground, sometimes to a height of nearly a metre. I ventured across the outside quadrangle just once and was immediately soaked through and nearly battered to the ground. After that I decided to stay put in the dining room and wait till the monsoon had stopped. After several hours it gradually lessened and finally abruptly stopped and we could immediately see the most glorious rainbow stretching across one end of the street. It seemed almost to beckon me towards it but I resisted its call and just enjoyed its beauty and extraordinarily vivid colours. It was now dusk and already becoming quite dark and the mosquitos were soon out in force and I sprayed myself all over and tried to cover up my arms as far as possible. Ripto told us that the malaria danger was extreme even for Indonesians and he also emphasised that the strain of mosquito in this area was virulent and that there might be no known antidote. Although he himself took no precautions I now felt much better about having brought the mosquito net with me. Later that night, after dinner and a short briefing by Rob Hall the expedition leader, I fastened it out around my bed and quickly slid underneath and made certain it was pulled tight around me. It felt hot and it was not easy to get to sleep underneath it but at least I felt much safer. I was also relaxed as, despite all my forebodings, I had made it halfway across the world and eventually joined up with the expedition team. It felt great and in spite of the buzzing of the mosquitos my sleep when it came was peaceful and untroubled.

The next morning we were all up early. I had a full breakfast and felt fully prepared for our journey into the heart of Irian Jaya. Our immediate group now totalled twelve expedition members plus Ripto, but there was also an enormous amount of luggage and so we had to split into two flight teams because of this. Fortunately I was put onto the first flight out along with Ripto, with Hall following on with the second team. We flew east, into the Maoke territory, dropping down across the Kobowre mountains, some with heights of up to 3,900 metres, across Lake Panial, over part of the Sudirman mountain range, over Banggelapa and Beoga, finally touching down at a tiny airstrip on the outskirts of the Ilaga village. Much further away eastwards was the main Dani town of Wamena, which was the usual starting out point for most travellers to explore the Baliem Valley and the regions around it.

As we came into land, out of the aircraft windows I caught my first glimpse of the extraordinary Danis; it was an enthralling sight and I was filled with wonderment. The men came rushing towards the aircraft even before it had finished taxiing, waving their spears and gesticulating wildly, black, tight curly hair, their skins also completely jet black, naked apart from their penis gourds (horim), all initially appearing extremely intimidating. Fortunately they proved to be just the opposite and were friendly, delightful, easy to approach, extremely curious themselves, very enthusiastic about everything and always willing to help. They

insisted on carrying our baggage out of the aircraft and across to
where a cleared section had been set aside, next to the helicopter
landing site. They chattered gaily away to us although we couldn't
understand them at all, but fortunately our Indonesian guides
could interpret mostly and soon we were exchanging all kinds of
information. The Danis had been headhunters and cannibals up
to only a few years previously and we were told by our guides
there were still some mysterious customs carried out deep within
the jungle, about which it was probably better we had no
knowledge. The women were also bare-chested but wore tiny,
grass skirts and when standing next to the men with their waving
horim the Dani people portrayed a picture of a long-lost world
into which we had stumbled by chance. The gourds were in all
kinds of shapes and sizes and were very impressive looking. After
the Danis had helped us unload the aircraft, which also had food
supplies for the Ilaga village, it took off back to Nabire, leaving
us in that most remote area, alone now only with the Danis who
of course vastly outnumbered us. It would be the last we would
see of it until we returned here after our journey to the mountains.
One helicopter only, instead of the 3 booked originally, had been
chartered to ferry us to another small landing strip and we settled
down to await its arrival. I was thrilled and absolutely fascinated
at last to come face to face with the Danis, took many photographs
and tried my best to exchange greetings and messages. They knew
no English and although at first were difficult to communicate
with, I persevered and they quickly responded with huge smiles
and peals of laughter. I couldn't get enough of these wonderful
people and over the period of the expedition and even after I
returned to England I learned as much about them as I could.
They seemed as curious to learn about us, as I was to know more
about them and this suited me just fine. I was happy to sit with
them and observe the way they behaved and they seemed content
for me to be with them.

Eventually the helicopter arrived and its pilot announced that
it could only carry two people additionally with him at any one
time and some three or four back-packs or other luggage. This
meant it would be a long and laborious process in moving the
whole team from here to the next camp site at the edge of the

jungle. This could delay us one day and we might miss our rendezvous with the part of the team that had trekked out earlier. We were allotted boarding positions and I waited patiently, sitting with the Danis and listening to their excited chatter, until it was my turn. When it was I scrambled quickly to the allotted spot, crouched down very low and waited until the helicopter had landed and the rotor blades ceased whirling. Still crouching low I ran forward and clambered quickly into the rear seat. One of the largest Americans, David Taylor a plastic surgeon, followed me and climbed into the front seat next to the pilot. There were a number of petrol drums close by on the strip and the pilot hurriedly used one of them to fill up the helicopter's fuel tanks. I clipped on the seat belt and safety buckles and put on the cans (headphones) to try and reduce the noise and air pressure. The noise as we took off was still tremendous. The helicopter sped through the air and I was able to look out over extremely dense jungle and exotic bush country, at one time with us passing directly over a group of Dani huts. They were built in simple round shapes, looking like giant, wild mushrooms from the air. I could see the Danis waving up at us and waved back although I guessed they couldn't see me.

After 40 minutes or so the helicopter banked, circled once around and then landed on a cleared, flat, hard earth area which I later learned was the only one possible in this whole region. From now on we would have to proceed only on foot. We waited until the pilot gave the all-clear signal and then quickly clambered out of our seats, at the same time also pulling with us the bags and packs from in the back. Again crouching very low we carried them over to the camp site some 30 metres away. Although we were positioned well below the helicopter's rotor blades, gusting winds could easily cause them to dip suddenly, so it was absolutely necessary to be very careful and to keep our heads down low and move as far away as fast as possible. At all times it was essential to remain in eye contact with the pilot, therefore one should never move across the rear of the helicopter, so the pilot could always see what was happening and could signal to us if necessary. We stacked the baggage and back-packs with those the others had already brought out, on the perimeter of the site and waited

patiently until the pilot had climbed back on board and taken
off again. Unfortunately my own back-pack was not amongst
those that had been brought out and therefore I didn't have any
warm clothes to put on; the temperature was already starting to
drop and rain was falling intermittently. It was unwise to set up
any of the tents until the helicopter had finished its rounds for
the day, as the turbulence caused by it's rotor blades would have
blown them away. The expedition leader, Rob Hall, had been
taken out in the first drop and so was with us. He had initially
made radio contact with his wife, Jan Arnold, the expedition
doctor who had trekked ahead with those of the Dani porters
carrying the heavier equipment, baggage and the food stores. Since
then however he had not been able to re-establish radio contact
and had hoped we would have been able to meet up with her and
the porters today but this now seemed very unlikely. Rob asked
if anyone wanted to see if they could locate Jan and the porters
and Dave Taylor said he would go. For safety reasons Rob
thought that at least two of us should go together, so I volunteered
to go with him. Taylor is a very experienced mountaineer and
had climbed Everest and also last year had travelled to Indonesia
to climb Carstensz Pyramid. Unfortunately the weather
conditions then on the mountain were so bad that none of that
team had been able to make the summit.

He and I set off initially across the open terrain, but soon we
had plunged deeper into some dense bush leading into the jungle
and after trekking for some while came to a tumbling, frothy
creek. We crossed over it by hopping onto the stones protruding
from its bed, although the water still splashed over and into our
boots. After that we climbed up a steep, mossy bank and headed
on further through the jungle, battling through its dense foliage.
After about an hour I thought that, as we hadn't come across Jan
Arnold and the Danis, it would be preferable to head back before
we got too far away from the camp site. Dave decided he wanted
to go on, particularly as he knew the terrain from his last trip. I
felt somewhat in a quandary about his decision and leaving him,
although he was quite happy to go on, but I decided to head back
anyhow. I tried to follow the path we had taken but soon got
confused as the terrain all around was so similar. I knew we had

crossed the creek and after I found it again decided to follow along its bank as far as possible, as hopefully I would find the place we had crossed it and could then head back towards the camp. It was always extremely difficult to stay close to the bank as the ground was very marshy and several times I had to clamber around the wet, boggy gorse and push through the thick bushes as best I could. I could not tell when or where there were holes under the prickly vegetation covering most of the ground, quite often I put a foot through it into holes full of water beneath and soon both my feet were soaking wet. After some time I found my way back to the camp and explained the position to Hall, but he wasn't worried about Taylor as he knew how experienced he was. After another hour Taylor finally re-appeared and very fortunately had met up with Jan Arnold's group and explained where they were. This was excellent news, Rob Hall was particularly delighted and soon we were able to establish radio contact again.

The weather was worsening all the time, the light was fading fast and we guessed by now there was no chance of the rest of the team and the remaining baggage getting out to us today. During the previous helicopter drops my own back-pack hadn't been brought out and presumably was still left behind at the Ilaga landing strip. This meant that all I had with me to keep the rain off was a bright yellow, plastic cape which my young daughter had proudly given me. I had taken it primarily out of sentiment but now in these wet conditions it proved to be extremely useful as a cover. When we realised the pilot had finally decided it was too dark and he would not risk any more runs and wouldn't be coming back again, we arranged to set up the tents. Although I didn't have my back-pack or bivi bag fortunately I did have my sleeping bag, which I had been allowed to carry with me on the helicopter. There was also one spare tent and I set this up and made myself as warm and comfortable inside as possible. The guides cooked some soups, a strange mixture of spaghetti, beans and chilli, and I ate a double portion in the hope this would help keep me warmer and I'd get through the cold night more easily. Inside the sleeping bag I kept all my clothes on, covered myself with everything I could and settled down to sleep and wait for morning light.

Lost In The Jungle

We were all up very early so we could take down the tents and have them packed up without delay. We expected the helicopter pilot would start ferrying in the rest of the team in as soon as it was fully light and we wanted to be ready. We heard its engine before it came into sight and over the next two hours the remaining expedition members and our baggage were safely landed. The helicopter took off again and once more we were on our own. On the final flight in my own back-pack arrived and I could at last take possession of it again. To give myself a special treat I changed into dry socks. At early daybreak the light had been dismal and grey, the air chilly and the skies seemed still full of the heavy rain that had fallen throughout the night, mostly preventing me from sleeping, although slightly easing off just before dawn. Now gradually the clouds disappeared and the sky brightened considerably, to be pierced by streaks of strong sunlight, with widening patches of blue appearing as the clouds dissolved. Eventually the light was almost too bright to bear. The sky became a moving mass of changing colours, sometimes gradating shades of brilliant vibrant reds, even deep purples and then again to quite extraordinary prussian blues.

Some of the expedition members had already decided to trek off to the next camp site in order to meet up with Jan Arnold and her group. Initially I stood and watched them, strung out in a long thin line before vanishing into the bush and undergrowth some distance ahead. As more left the camp and started trekking out, I started to become concerned I might be left too far behind and I asked Hall if I should join up with them and could set off as well. He agreed but advised me to keep in close contact with the others and of course I intended to. The next set of climbers had their packs on and were already moving out so I rushed over to join them. This meant I didn't have time to change into shorts or anything lighter and I was still wearing most of the heavier clothes I'd worn during the night, although I had packed my jacket. It was already quite hot and I soon realised I was very over-dressed. However I didn't want to stop, in case I lost contact with the others who were already some 10 or more metres ahead and seemed to be trekking on at a hard and fast pace. I was starting not to feel well and presumed I had probably overeaten on the previous night. Whoever cooked the meal had put in all kinds of different sauces with the spaghetti until it was a complete mixture and, coming on top of the thick Spanish vegetable soup I had eaten to begin with, it obviously hadn't settled too well and my stomach was starting to complain bitterly. It was hard to maintain a reasonable pace and soon I realised I was dropping far behind.

Before long I was feeling more and more unwell and very hot and desperately wanted to rest. I wished I could remove some of my clothes but was worried about stopping and possibly losing contact with those who were now some considerable way ahead of me. I found myself gradually slowing and was trailing more and more behind and eventually I just couldn't continue. I shouted out to Doug Mantle, one of the many American climbers, who was a number of metres ahead, that I was going to stop and change down and would follow on as quickly as I could. He shouted back he would keep an eye out for me but that was the last I saw of him during that day. Louis Bowen, another American but now living in Singapore, then caught up with me and asked which was the way we were meant to follow. I explained that I'd last seen Mantle trekking on some way ahead and that he'd then cut sharply over to the left, plunging directly into the jungle where presumably there was some kind of path to follow. That seemed a little strange to both of us as we could see the mountains were well over to our right, but we guessed somewhere along the trail there would be a turn-off then leading us through towards the mountains. I told Bowen I'd follow on very soon and he nodded and moved on. I watched him strike out also left into the jungle and quickly vanish from sight.

I was feeling weaker and very hot and undressed and changed into a T-Shirt and shorts and then started slowly after him. Within a few metres I felt even more feverish and unwell and had to stop to rest for some moments. I tried to keep moving but was finding it more and more difficult and eventually I had no choice but to lie down in the jungle. Suddenly I was violently sick. After some moments of just lying down, my head completely bathed with sweat, I tried to get up but was immediately sick again and this occurred several times. I had continued to take my anti-malarial tablets and some of the team members had thought this was unwise, particularly in this hot and humid atmosphere and I thought this also might have made me sick. I doubted if this was really the case and presumed it was probably a combination of overeating, not enough sleep, becoming too hot and moving off too fast. I was feeling so bad that I couldn't get up for some while and just lay in the grass and undergrowth listening to the sounds of the jungle around me. Oddly enough that was quite pleasant and soothing and I was okay provided I didn't try to get up. Each time I did I just collapsed in a heap and my mind almost blanked out. I wondered if it was an opportunity to meditate and that might pull me together but it proved impossible as my mind kept wandering. I could feel the light breaking through the trees and dancing around me. No one else from the expedition passed me and I didn't know whether this meant I had wandered off the path, they had taken another route or some were still back at the camp site and had yet to leave.

After some considerable time I partly recovered and felt able to move off again, albeit very slowly. I was still feeling feverish but realised I had also lost my bearings and now I wasn't really certain which direction to follow. I trekked slowly to the left for a while further but just found myself moving into denser and thicker jungle. This meant I had to change my directions several times and I knew I was becoming more lost by the minute and I was still feeling extremely weak but knew somehow I had to continue. I came to a creek and hoped it might be the one I had crossed the previous day. This time I didn't have the strength and energy to leap across the stones and waded through it and then started to clamber up the slopes on the other side.

The undergrowth soon became even denser and there were all kinds of holes and gullies, some obvious, others hidden within it. I missed my footing several times and eventually fell totally over, straining my right leg in the process. I finally came to a rest against a rotting tree trunk, almost semi-conscious from several cracks on the head. I lay there breathless for some moments trying to gauge if there had been any real damage or whether it was only superficial. All of a sudden I realised I was staring at a strangely-curved twig and the twig was actually staring at me; it had an eye. It didn't blink and just stared directly back at me, but I couldn't tell whether it really saw me or whether perhaps to it I didn't exist. It looked like no other creature or insect I had ever seen or even heard of before. As I tried to focus more fully and examine it in detail it vanished. One moment it was there, the next moment it had gone. I hadn't seen it tense itself or move, it had been too fast for the human eye. Yet I had seen it, for a brief few moments and had known it. I had only seen the one eye. Did it have two? Were there creatures with only one eye. Cyclops of the insect and animal kingdoms. Why not. Was it necessary to have two eyes, two hands, two legs for that matter. I was in a jungle where many of, if not most of its creatures had never been catalogued. Perhaps I had indeed seen something that had never been seen before. Was I hallucinating from the fall. I shook my head to clear my mind more fully but I felt very wide awake. I had seen it and its one eye, we had definitely made eye contact. I tried to recall every detail I could, its colouring, markings, the shape and size, but above everything else that one eye protruded itself into my recollection, an eye that was too large in proportion to its sloping, curved green-brown head. I decided to name it, to give it yet further existence and immediately the name Darwin seemed the most appropriate. I started to wonder why the father of the evolutionary theory, certainly to my knowledge, had never had a creature named after him. Was Charles Darwin too illustrious a name for just a single creature. Did he deserve a whole species, perhaps he deserved a galaxy even. Anyhow now there was a stick insect, possibly with just one eye, in the depths of the Irian Jaya jungle, called Darwin. For a brief, confusing moment I wondered if I should have called it Satori but that was too heavy a thought at that moment and so Darwin it remained. I eased myself gently to my feet brushing off the leaves and twigs sticking to me, conscious very much that amongst them could be another Darwin or even another previously unknown creature. But if there was one I didn't see it.

The brambles and thistle were continually tearing at my bare arms and legs and I was getting cuts all over. After I had taken a second tumble I lay there for a moment, again completely winded, but fully conscious now of the painful scratches and grazes all across my arms and legs. It was just so much easier to lie there, not having to struggle up and to continue. I was lying in a deep patch of thick vegetation, very coarse and prickly, but although it was causing me some pain this was dulled by the heavier pains I felt in both my legs, particularly my right one, where I had wrenched it badly when tripping and falling earlier. Anyhow I needed to regain my breath for a little bit longer and so I lay there looking up through the foliage of the trees towards the ultra-bright sky that glimmered and pirouetted through the myriad branches above me. There is the Zen saying, 'Knock on the sky and listen to the sound'. That was very calming but in a way it was also dangerous, as it lulled me into a feeling of relaxation and composure and I could feel I was starting to lose the desire to fight and struggle on. One of the most important rules of the jungle is also to hear with the eyes, see with the ears, to be totally aware in all ways within your surroundings. The wind through the branches caused a kind of whistling and hissing sound. It was as if I was being overlooked by thousands of creatures, although not in an hostile way, but watching me only out of curiosity, even though they were not able to assist in any way. I was totally on my own. A Zen koan asks, 'When the Many are reduced to One, to what is the One reduced?' It was only my thoughts and the will they contained which existed at that exact moment.

There were so many colours in the trees above me, all kinds of hues and shades, creating countless shapes and shadows, that I started to feel stronger just by the inspiration of the multiplicity of the nature concentrated in that one tiny area. The natural forces they created were so strong that I felt as if there were laser beams piercing directly into my mind, although incapable of finding ways through or out. I became completely conscious of my own body, its aches and pains in so many different places and yet that didn't really matter, all that mattered was that I was alive and I had a chance, even many chances and it was up to me to take them. Life is very much like that; there are always chances, always opportunities, it is really up to the individual to seize them, no matter how dire or dangerous the situation may seem.

You always have to go for it and accept nothing is totally impossible. Whether it was the fever, the hot sun beating down, hallucination or the strangeness of where I was, I started to feel I was very much within a lost world. This led my thoughts to Sir Arthur Conan Doyle's The Lost World, his most exciting adventure book, then to his Sherlock Holmes stories, perennial favourites of mine and that wonderful Zen-like exposition that is forever Holmes, 'When you have dealt with the impossible, then the improbable, no matter how improbable, only remains and is the truth'. I wasn't certain if those were the exact words but I knew they were his sentiments. Holmes' aesthetic flashes of exquisite mental clarity and inspiration were fine counterpoints to the loyal, dogged resilience of Dr. Watson, surely one of the most magnificent literary couplings. Some doggedness was what I required at this particular moment. Out of the blue I also recalled the rather odd fact that it was Conan Doyle who had once, well before Palestine became the front runner, suggested that New Guinea should be the new Jewish homeland. Now here I was, virtually lost in the jungles of New Guinea. I felt moved by these connections and coincidences, although Sai Baba, one of the most well-known Indian Swamis, explains that there are no such things as coincidences; he always refers to them as God's incidences. The strength I took from that thought gave me the power and courage to pull myself together and to set off again.

I knew I must keep going, even through I was aware how easy it was for travellers to lose their sense of direction and to circle round and round, often coming back to exactly the same starting point again and again. Somehow I didn't think I would and I was determined now to keep my sense of direction and trek on in more or less a straight line. This was however subject to the numerous ambushes I came to in reaching many impassable parts of the forest, although always eventually seeing a gap through and finding a way ahead to follow. Unfortunately I couldn't always be certain it would lead anywhere especially, but it was there and I felt compelled to follow it. There was always a Zen koan which was apposite and again I reached into my mental Zen notebook, 'The way is beneath your feet'. Impossible as it had first seemed because of the dense and tangled brambles that kept blocking me, I now finally got myself into some kind of rhythm. I was able to make some steady progress, stepping forward, pulling aside the lowest branches, sometimes ducking under them, yet trying to make certain that each foot would not plunge into some hole or warren that might trap it and pull me down. One of the great dangers would be to rick an ankle or twist a leg as this might easily prevent me making it through to-day and subsequently on the mountains.

The jungle was alive with sound, all kinds of rustling noises, flickering lights and sudden movements. I couldn't tell whether they were made by different forest creatures or were only echoes from the wind or just the sounds of the trees and the bushes. Mostly though I found the sounds very comforting, even inspiring and exciting, although occasionally there would be the one or two ominous noises that I felt might represent something more dangerous or hostile. I knew there were snakes in the forest but so far hadn't seen any and of course I hoped that I wouldn't. I didn't have too much fear of them, other than in experiencing a direct confrontation, this knowledge coming out of my journeys many years ago into the Amazonas in South America. I had learned that snakes were not necessarily to be feared and there were in fact only a few really venomous or dangerous snakes to avoid. Some of the mystic religions use them as symbols of rebirth because they shed their skins. In Roman times snakes were looked on favourably and were incorporated into their statues to symbolise the spirit. Some people do suffer badly from ophidophobia but snakes as a rule will not attack, except mostly in defence. Therefore I mainly had to hope that I wouldn't tread upon a snake asleep or coiled within its nest. I knew that if a snake heard me coming invariably it would try to move away and out of my path. The thought though actively crossed my mind that if I should eventually need food I might actually be looking for a snake to kill and then would need to try and cook it over a fire. My skills in this field were rather limited but I guessed that I could do it if I really had to; I only prayed that I wouldn't. At least my friend Ray Mears, the survival expert, had shown me some of his firelighting skills.

My thoughts were continually racing, full of so many different ideas and things, but nothing to do with the trappings of civilisation, aeroplanes, cars, trains, computers; there was so much else to occupy me and the feel of the wind and the wildness about me was wonderfully all-consuming. I actually felt rather content, even happy, in these strange, isolated and solitary conditions. The instinct of self-preservation obviously meant that I had to find a way out, a way through the jungle, but it was no longer so paramount that it created a feeling of fear or panic. Perhaps that is why I was so easily able to continue and to marshall those thoughts and energies I needed in order to fight against any obstacles Nature intended to impose. In its way I felt it was not laying down a mighty challenge but mostly tussling, almost playing with me, in a way enabling me to use my Zen and draw on my inner resources; but always allowing me to make sufficient headway, achieve some degree of success, so as not to cause me to feel too dispirited or defeated. I knew that negativity was the one thing that would defeat me.

Occasionally I'd disturb the nesting of a quail, a pheasant, or a grouse as I trekked on. Whatever it was would shoot out of the grasses with an almighty flurry, as if trying to avoid my seeing where its nest or cover was, startling me just as presumably I had startled it. It seemed a terrible although necessary thought, but again I knew if I couldn't find my way out quickly, it meant that at least there was something else I might need to try and kill in order to survive that much longer. I so much hoped that that wouldn't be the case, doubting that I'd have the ability to stalk and capture one before it flew away. At least that possibility existed and it was another way of my retaining hope and fighting against any despair. Often I could hear the sound of water, as there were a number of streams gushing their way throughout the jungle and I knew I'd always be able to find plenty of water and that thirst would certainly not be any problem. I also had my purifying tablets with me and whenever I stopped to fill up my water bottles I still conscientiously dropped in the two tablets and waited the several minutes for them to evaporate and hopefully purify the water. It was perhaps odd, in those rather desperate circumstances, where my life was at risk, that I still took and followed those elementary safety precautions, but I was aware that to become sick or infected in the jungle would certainly reduce my chances. Although uncertain of the way ahead I didn't want to stop and felt I must keep going at all costs, to find a path leading out of the jungle or even stumble across the actual trail I needed.

Eventually the realisation sunk in that I was absolutely lost within the jungle and that really I had no idea how to proceed. I had sufficient water and food to last several days so at least I had no worries on that score. I realised that if I didn't find a path soon I was going to become more and more lost and that eventually it would be extremely difficult, if not impossible, for anyone subsequently to come and find me; of course no one would probably realise I was missing until very late that evening, after everyone else had reached camp. They then obviously would not be able to do anything that night, because of the early darkness, but hopefully the next morning, probably by radio, would be able to ask for a helicopter and someone would be sent out to look for me. Calmness was certainly the order of the moment. Within Zen a great emphasis is always laid on simplicity in thought and action, exercising at all times self-control; being fully aware of every moment and behaving with tranquillity in the face of adversity or even death. I couldn't have found a more absolute test than this.

The foliage and jungle plants were so thick that at times I really needed a machete to cut them and often I had to tear at the branches and bushes with my hands and force them apart to find a way through. Having travelled so deeply into the jungle, itself set within a valley, I now had no idea of the right way to proceed and I decided that the only thing to do was to climb up as high as I could and reach some vantage point. I came to a densely wooded slope and toiled my way up to its top ridge, but when I reached it it was still not high enough to see anything in any direction, I needed to climb even higher. The only thing to do was to climb over this ridge and then down again into the next valley and try to find a higher ridge.

I was feeling extremely tired and decided before moving on I had to rest for a few moments. However I knew I must keep my mind active and must not fall asleep otherwise I could lose the will to continue. To keep myself alert I recalled I had read previously about a special test used for jungle and native peoples and I tried to remember exactly how it was organised. It is called the Lowenfeld Mosaic Test. It is aimed at evaluating tribal peoples throughout the world, to show how they go about similar tasks, then comparing the results and trying to analyze them. It is used in psychological and cultural analyses particularly and also in cross-cultural comparisons. A set of 228 tiles (wood, or plastic) is provided in six different colours, white, green, black, yellow, blue and red; five different shapes, square, equilateral triangle, diamond, isosceles triangle, scalene triangle. They should then be arranged on a board or flat surface in whatever manner the person being tested decides. No hints are given regarding the possibilities of any arrangements, whether they should be placed one next to another, on top of each other or perhaps fitted together as in a jigsaw. Some people design houses, other birds, flowers, human figures, but it seems very few ever create abstract items. I learned later that the Danis, like the other Irian Jaya tribes, only really worked in a three dimensional way and did not understand two dimensional objects. Assuming I found my way out, I thought I would like to try this kind of test on the Danis and also some of the other climbers but there never was the opportunity and anyhow I didn't have the tiles, so I never did.

It was time to trek on. I fought through the brambles as fast as I could and worked my way down to the bottom of the hill. Then I had no choice but to trek across the narrow valley section and climb the next ridge I reached. I only hoped this time it would be high enough. I battled through the thick and exotic foliage, not now having the time even to stop and admire the beauty of some quite exquisite plants I was coming across. I was worried about calling out in order to try and attract anyone's attention. Although, when I met them at the landing strip, the Dani tribesmen had seemed extremely friendly and easygoing I was then in a group of some 20 or so and there did not seem to be any danger. Now, on my own, if they came across me I wondered if they would be quite as friendly. I vividly remembered that they had only officially stopped being cannibals a few years back and perhaps on my own I might prove more of a temptation. Anyhow I was still feeling pretty weak and needed to conserve my energies and for the time being I decided not to shout out.

Eventually I fought my way to the top of the next ridge and fortunately this time was able to see over the top of the jungle and there over to the far right was a range of mountains. I had to presume that these were the ones we had come to climb; I could only hope there was not another range in another direction I couldn't see. This meant that I had to climb and trek back most of the way I had already come but there was no other choice. I clambered down the ridge to the valley floor, across it and up to the top of the next ridge, down the other side again, all the time fighting through the brambles and bushes, in the direction of those mountains, trying to keep in my mind's eye where they were sited. I was extremely tired, still feeling feverish and I desperately wanted to stop and rest but I knew that it would be dangerous to do so. It could become dark very suddenly and then it would be almost impossible, even using a torch, to find my way through the jungle. I felt strange, completely lost within the jungle, totally on my own, trapped within this remote land, searching earnestly for a way out, where even the greatest spiritual revelation would be of little use to me if time itself ran out.

After I had climbed and continued on for some considerable time I finally decided I must risk calling out and try to contact someone. I stopped and I shouted out several times but there was no response. My voice seemed to echo forlornly back at me. I trekked on, now stopping every 10 or 20 metres to shout out and to listen for any response but there was nothing. I realised the denseness of the foliage was helping to blanket out the sound of my voice and probably it could only travel a short distance. It seemed so ironic. I had come all this way to climb two very difficult mountains, with limited climbing technique and experience; yet, instead of those mountains being the problems, I was now faced with the greater danger of being lost within the jungles of Irian Jaya. I felt more than a little feverish, I was sweating profusely, my head hurting, all parts of my body aching. I wondered whether each jungle was different or were all jungles the same. Certainly they all had the same power and primitive magic to overwhelm you, to intrude deep into your inner recesses and to take a hold of your mind, in a way which was incomprehensible to the city dweller. Here the jungle had the ultimate power. There were mysteries here, all kinds of strange things, many of which I could only guess at and would never know, perhaps no one would ever know. It was almost too much to comprehend, the intensity of it all was overpowering and yet at the same time I felt immensely privileged. There was so much ancient history in the jungle, tribal customs, primitive feelings and emotions, which the jungle contained and owned and which if I allowed could easily envelope me.

Perhaps it was part of the fever I felt, but I found myself journeying back in time, many years ago, to my first visit to the Ecuadorian jungles and rain forests, travelling on a boat with my family taking us deep into the Amazonas. It was New Year's Eve, just before midnight and time to welcome in the New Year. There was only a single lantern light on the boat and on the banks of the Amazon River there were the lights of several small fires that had been set ablaze. Suddenly, as we cruised to a stop, out of the jungle came three or four figures dragging someone dressed in women's clothes, seemingly resisting and protesting but being dragged closer and closer to one of the fires. There were shouts of encouragement from the boatmen, echoed by shouts and cries from the jungle; there was a flurry of movement and bodies and the woman was suddenly pushed shrieking into the fire, to perish and to be consumed. We quickly learned of course that it was not a real person, but only a bundle of rags that had been thrown upon the fire but it had seemed initially to be a human body. There were more screams as 'the figure' blazed and incinerated in a cloud of billowing smoke. It was later explained that one of the boatmen had dressed up as a woman to represent the spirit of the outgoing year and was being burnt on the fire in order to welcome in and encourage the New Year to be a good one. Somehow his woman's clothes were removed or others substituted and thrown on the fire, but in that magical moment it had seemed to be so very real. I remembered that I had never seen so many sparkling stars shining so very brightly as on that night and the light they provided contrasted so strongly with the impenetrable darkness of the surrounding jungle. It was an extraordinary moment, but it had occurred in another jungle, in another part of the world, in another time and I was now here, in Indonesia, in the jungles of Irian Jaya and I must find a way through.

In Irian Jaya and in the neighbouring Papua New Guinea there are some of the most inhospitable regions in the world, mostly untracked and unmapped and very little visited or explored. In fact there had been media reports earlier in the year about an army team that had been lost in Low's Gully, in Papua New Guinea although of course they were a team with back-up facilities, whereas I was totally on my own. I crossed over another small creek and wondered whether it was the same one I had crossed previously although it seemed so very long ago. A huge, gorgeous butterfly with vibrant flamboyant colours and movements fluttered briefly around my head, perhaps this was one being seen for the first time, at least by a non-Indonesian. Certainly I was the first Englishman the butterfly had seen, if indeed it even noticed me. I knew there were over 18,000 species of butterflies in the world and wondered how many were to be found within the archipelago of Indonesia, how many lived in the jungles and lowlands of Irian Jaya. There were so many unexplored areas here, surely there must be many butterfly species still undiscovered. A butterfly's time is so fleeting but so important. The Japanese poet Buson expressed it so exquisitely when he wrote in three lines: The butterfly - Resting upon the temple bell - Asleep. Haiku is the shortest form of poetry known in world literature. Haiku is not Zen although Zen can be said to be haiku.

I was now shouting out more and more often to try and attract attention, but there was still no response. Suddenly I thought I heard something. I stopped, waited, shouted again but could hear nothing more. I plunged urgently on through the foliage, all the time trying to make certain that I was heading towards the distant mountain range. I shouted out once more and this time I definitely heard a voice answering, it sounded like 'Yahoo!' Of course I had no idea who it might be or whether indeed it was one of the

Dani tribesmen but felt I had no real choice but to trek towards the sound. I pushed on furiously and finally was much relieved to hear a voice calling out in English. It turned out to be an American, John Regis (an Aspen ski instructor no less) who together with another colleague Alan Tarnley had been taking a more leisurely route. That was very fortunate for me and I was extremely thankful to meet up with them and I gratefully explained my predicament and briefly what had occurred. They could see how unwell I still was and kindly agreed to trek more slowly with me. Regis asked if I'd met up with the Danis or any other tribesmen whilst I was lost. When I replied I hadn't, he confirmed how lucky that probably was. He'd heard a number of stories of people disappearing in the jungle and never being seen again, with everyone imagining they'd been taken by headhunters or come to an equally unpleasant end. I knew from my experiences how easily the jungle could swallow someone up and as a relief offered the following story: Two cannibals were in the middle of eating a clown. One stopped and said to the other 'You know, I can taste something funny'. Tarnley burst out laughing, fit to burst, at this and throughout the rest of the expedition repeated it to everyone he could, himself above all the others roaring loudly with laughter each time. I hadn't thought of it as being so amusing and could only hope none of the Danis ever overheard or understood him. Together the three of us finally found the correct trail and after several hours of painful and exhausting trekking, at least for me, reached the camp site.

I met Rob Hall's wife, Dr. Jan Arnold, who was also acting as the team doctor and explained briefly what had occurred. She immediately asked if I suffered from altitude sickness and of course I said 'No'. She also asked if I had any fever or had a headache and I again replied, 'No', though in fact I did have one. If I had admitted any of this I was concerned she might immediately put my being unwell down to suffering from altitude sickness. I knew this would count against me, either immediately or later on and there was always a possibility she might prevent me continuing with the expedition. We had now reached a height of approximately 3,500 metres and I knew that certainly over 3,000 metres a number of people suffer from altitude sickness. I explained to her that I was just feeling sick, probably from something I had eaten the night before and that I would soon recover and she should not worry about me at all. She advised me to stop taking the anti-malarial tablets, as she considered they could make me sick and stated anyhow they were not effective against the strain of mosquitoes found in these areas. She also said that it was not really necessary to use the purifying tablets when using water from any of the streams. As I preferred to err on the side of caution privately I decided I would continue to take the malaria tablets and still use the purifying tablets. But of course I didn't try to argue these matters through with her. To allow myself to recover I didn't eat any food that evening and merely sipped at some black tea throughout the night. Luckily I was soon starting to feel somewhat better, although still rather weak. I also met again Louis Bowen who, although he had continued on before me, had also got lost. Fortunately for him he had subsequently met up with one of the other climbers who knew the way, so that the two of them had been able to work their way through the jungle and reach the camp site earlier. Ripto told me this area is known as Nasi Domeh. His delightful but quaint enunciation made the words sound more like Nessun Dorma, but in this case I expected that tonight everyone would be able to sleep, particularly me. I felt so very contented finally to be here with the other expedition members. It had been such a long tiring day but I was no longer lost in the jungle and I was at peace. Gradually I felt myself relaxing into the beautiful jungle night. Somewhere out there a lone forest bird trilled out a short, plaintive song before it too fell silent.

Reaching The Dani Cavern

We started trekking out early from camp although already a fierce, draining heat was starting to build. I was soon breathing hard, not feeling at all confident and straining to match the fast pace set by those leading. The way up the rocks quickly became steep and very muddy. My boots were soon sinking deep into the mud and I continually had to fight to pull them out. We then started climbing up a series of razor-sharp rocks which took a considerable amount of intricate balancing to avoid slipping off them. If you toppled over there was every chance of gashing yourself badly on their sharp and jagged edges. Some of the other climbers were finding it even more difficult than I was and there were several mishaps. The climb continued steeply upwards, long and laborious and I tried to develop a rhythm to cope with it. After reaching the final section we had to trek through several wide clefts cut into the vaulted valley walls. We followed the stream which had breached one of the walls and was spilling down from the rock tops, spouting foam and rainbow sprays in all directions. Throughout the day I used my Zen techniques to get me through. Practising Zen in the sitting position is called zazen, but in walking, trekking and any physical activity, it is called kinhin. Throughout kinhin it is also vital to follow the practice of breathing correctly, as well as practising hishiryo which is creating a state of thought without thinking, allowing your consciousness to expand beyond normal thought.

One of the Dani porters, making light of the tremendous weight he was carrying, a bulky and large rucksack balanced firmly on his head, easily passed me. He seemed to prefer carrying it this way, rather than holding it by wearing straps tied around his shoulders as most of the others were. We climbed past some sweet potato fields stretched out on the lower slopes and the women there, helped or hindered by their squealing but eager pigs, were digging away at the mud with curved sticks and hauling out purple tubers. The sweet potato certainly grows everywhere and is obviously the cornerstone of Dani life in and around these valleys. No one seems to know how the sweet potato got to Irian Jaya though of course there are many stories and explanations. One is that it only arrived in the 17th century after the Portuguese discovered it in Peru and brought it into Asia. Another is that it had arrived even nine hundred years earlier than that. This could be the reason why the Danis had expanded their territory beyond the valleys themselves and opened up the land on the higher areas, as the sweet potato could easily cling to the mountainside. This could mean it had been brought there by Polynesian seamen which would indicate that they had travelled way beyond Easter Island and probably made it all the way across to Peru. They would have traded with the native indians in order to obtain the sweet potato from them. Whatever the correct reason it was certainly now in Irian Jaya in abundance.

We passed several compounds of Dani huts, many shaped like old-fashioned beehives, with their straw thatch reaching almost down to the ground. They were often surrounded by long, low barns, shaped somewhat like triangular haystacks, possibly 10 metres in length. Inside each hut there was always a fire with blue and white smoke spiralling freely through the centre of the thatch. One woman came out of her hut to stare at us, a little pig snapping at her heels and when she rubbed her cheek I stared directly and rather rudely back as I could see that her left hand was totally fingerless. She would have lost many relatives and carried out the mourning tradition of each time removing one finger. Each of the compounds had a kitchen garden with mounds of cabbages, taro, potatoes covering the ground. There was a rich black soil, its richness the complete opposite of the very poor quality soil in the forest lowlands. They were also growing gourds on trellises outside the huts, some with stones tied to the gourds in an effort to make them grow longer and thinner. There were usually narrow, stone pig-runs beside the compounds. One of our Indonesian guides stopped to point out a ghost path set beside a woven fence, several of the sticks decorated with leaves and feathers designed in a special way. This was done in order to mislead the spirits into thinking they should go elsewhere and hopefully they would then miss the compound entirely. The Dani's old hut structures had originally been built with stone tools, or points and scrapers made from bone or bamboo; however the newer structures were made with the metal axes and knives which were now more readily available within the valley and the trading markets.

The trail had soon narrowed and we were climbing up again and soon reached another stream. This gradually became very much smaller, breaking into little water falls. We continued trekking up through the mottled hillsides and eventually reached a glorious flowery heath. There were wild, yellow rhododendron bushes contrasting vividly with the greens and greys of the coarse vegetation, all kinds of lichens and some bulbous blue flowers sprawling haphazardly along the ground. I even came across a few wild strawberries. Orchids of all kinds of varieties could be found everywhere, particularly on the banks of streams, so many and so gorgeous that many times I just had to stop in wonder. As I turned around the next corner, past some huge boulders, I disturbed an aggrieved creature which snorted and bristled furiously, before crashing off into the forest making loud, heavy and aggressive grunts. Presumably a large, black pig, although it looked and sounded like some evil, black devil. I was very pleased that it chose to run away from me rather than towards me. Down to the left, across a much larger, faster-flowing stream, there was a bridge, strung from rattan vines with a plank walkway and cane banisters woven into the sides. A Dani man and woman crossed it and passed by, the man giving me a cheery wave, his headband spread with parrot feathers; the young woman carrying a large number of sweet potatoes in the net bag (noken) hanging down her back, the thongs gripping tightly around her head although she seemed totally unaware of the weight.

Grey, thick clouds were fixed firmly to the hills ahead announcing the afternoon monsoon, but here it was still extremely hot and sticky. I was sweating profusely and I could feel the veins in my forehead throbbing with the effort I needed to continue. Apart from heat and tiredness there were always many other good reasons to stop and look around. Our trail led directly into the forest but then seemed immediately to peter out. 'The clearest way into the Universe is through a forest wilderness', the great woodsman, John Muir, had said so I didn't hesitate but resolutely pushed on. A sulphur-crested cockatoo, at a great height, was flapping around like an awkward moth high above the trees before perching at the top of the highest, bare branch. Many times I could hear the cries of cockatoos or other birds from within the forest, although there were few sightings. At one time though I heard a deep honking noise and was lucky enough to see, flying through a break in the trees, an immense black cockatoo, much larger than the white one, with a huge hooked nose that protruded down far below its chin. The forest floor was becoming more slippery by the minute. Most of the trees sat on spreading buttress roots and their trunks also seemed to sweat through skins of spines. Some of the paths had been worn away to expose the clay beneath. Occasionally a bird-winged butterfly fluttered past, often russet and white, sometimes captured briefly within a light spot beaming itself across our path. As quickly the butterfly would disappear into the darker shades of the forest and I always felt the loss.

After a while the forest became intermittent and we could see steaming patches of wet, bedraggled leaves glistening on the ground below us. Inside some of them there were white lilies or bunches of dusty and strange little, blue berries on top of thin stalks. They looked appetizing but I was told they could kill you so I certainly didn't dream of tasting them. I was drinking a great deal and my water was running low, so when I came across a small, marshy pond I stopped to fill my water bottle, still putting in the two sterilising tablets, as who could know what lurked beneath those dank waters. Suddenly one of our guides grabbed hold of me and pulled me back from the edge. He laughed loudly and pointed down and I could now see the swaying leeches that were just below the surface, and that had looked previously to me like dead leaves or twigs. I shuddered to think how close I had been to them and what it might have meant if they had managed to fix themselves onto my arms or legs. The guide flicked open his knife and slid its long, thin blade underneath one and lifted it to allow me a closer look. I backed away and he flicked the leech high into the air so it fell into the middle of the pond. I felt rather less keen about drinking the water from that pool, even with the sterilisation and hoped I'd find a cleaner and clearer pool shortly so I could replace it.

Without warning the rain came sizzling down and we were immediately soaked. We stripped off our shirts, the rain water bouncing in all directions, although myr skin still felt quite sweaty. The glistening water highlighted fruits that had fallen down around the path we were following, wild green mangoes, unrecognisable, mottled, grey lumpy things, speckled orange and red husks covered in prickles. None of them looked at all appetizing. A few of the Danis started to call out, presumably to make contact with other Danis ahead, but it was impossible to comprehend how the very strange noises sounded differently, although presumably they meant something to them. I was told there was a whole range of messages that could be passed on in this way. When it was raining heavily there would be rumbling noises resounding within the trees and this would cut out any low sounds, so the Danis would shriek in an extremely high and wild manner, as well as rolling their eyes as if to show how penetrating the cry had been. If there was no rain falling they would sometimes hit a buttress root with the side of a machete to make a huge thud. The Danis could also yodel in quite an extraordinary way, so that these sounds would carry even further. There were different yodels for the high and the low ground but although I heard them they all sounded more or less alike so that I couldn't tell any real difference.

The rain continued to fall heavily and without breaking them bounced through the masses of spiders' webs that were strung across the paths. The spiders were extraordinary looking, their bodies thick and warty, often pyramid-like in shape, in red and white enamel colours that gave them a more exotic menace than usual. One of the climbers inadvertently walked into a whole nest of them and started yelling as he tried to swipe them away and brush them out of his hair. Even when he was clear he couldn't stop shaking and told me he had always suffered from arachnophobia. For his sake I hoped we had seen the last of them, and decided not to tell him that the bites of all spiders are venomous, although luckily most are unable to pierce the skin. At the top of the trunk of one very high tree there was an enormous yellow and white orchid spreading out in all directions; haloed by the whitish sky above as the raindrops bounced around it, it was quite an extraordinary sight. Fortunately the rain soon eased and finally stopped and the sun broke through again. For some while we had been climbing up and making our way over broken rocks with tree roots that had grown and curved in amongst them. Various birds trilled out and suddenly a scarlet finch shot over our heads from its nesting hole which had been hidden in the nearby grasses. There were always all kinds of mysterious sounds to be heard. Usually I couldn't tell what they were, whether birds, forest creatures, frogs or even the Danis themselves shouting and trying to make contact. I heard a purring sound from a bush and as I stepped towards it a crowned pigeon came flustering out, flapping and making an enormous commotion as it hurriedly took off. Under a pile of leaves and dirt I would have ignored, a guide showed me, hidden within it, the nest mound of a maovo fowl, a bird somewhat like a turkey. Instead of sitting on their eggs to hatch, they always bury them deeply amongst the vegetation, rather like hiding them within a compost heap. The fowl is able to regulate the temperature by adding to or taking from the heap leaves and vegetation. I was also shown how the resins from the sandalwood trees could be tapped and lit in order to make a torch. The collected resins are dropped onto long, wrapped leaves and held in this way they can burn for several hours.

The path had become almost indistinct and we were constantly tripping on the roots and broken parts of trees that were strewn in all directions. There were plenty of orchid clusters, amazing pink and purple flowers in striking contrast to the deep green and bright yellow leaves, often brilliantly lit up by the sun. At one moment a flock of hornbills spectacularly took off, graceful black and white birds swishing past, their huge beaks held stiffly out ahead, but they were gone almost in a flash. I was constantly reminded that I was travelling within an area still practically unexplored, probably the most unknown place left in the world. There are so many strange birds, exotic creatures and animals here which are still to be recorded; so many isolated valleys and inaccessible swamps that almost anything could be living there, undetected perhaps for centuries by anyone from the outside world. Huge fish are continually being discovered within the lakes but there are also connecting rivers, some of them underground, which have never been visited, maybe they never will be. Some mysteries will remain forever.

We were now trekking through a lengthy, sandy-floored forest of dried pines. Abruptly it changed to become a humid, peaty jungle with a few birds only briefly glimpsed through the shafts of light and meaty toadstools and exotic flowers occasionally picked out against the green moss. Walking was becoming a real problem as the ground was extremely soggy. Because of this some trees had been felled previously and lined up to enable anyone to clamber across them; this was much easier for the Danis with their large, flat feet but the soles of our boots often slipped. Several times my boots sank into mud pools which were edging the sides of the tree trunks. This went on for some while and became extremely tiring. I was certainly pleased when finally the track cut sharply upwards and out of the peat mud. Suddenly we were in a different world entirely. The glacial plains were spread before us, bare and windswept, miles of small gritty stones and low yellowed grasses. A bitterly cold wind cut sharply across us and we could hear it echoing away down through the rocks. There were also clumps of tree ferns, black, silent, perhaps dating back originally half a billion years. We had moved back in time again and we were traversing an old world and yet through part of the new world at the same time.

We threaded our way across the plains towards the lowest of the mountain slopes, ringed by forest clumps. We came across thorny scrubland, bog pools, high grasses, from which brown thorn-living birds flew out inquisitively to study us. In the distance I could clearly see the enormous mountain of Carstensz Pyramid, composed of rock ledges and false summits, reaching to its fearsome summit ridge of sheer cold-grey rock. We ourselves had now reached only around 3,400 metres, but the air continued to thin and every effort required was enormous. The twisting pathways were often amazing combinations of colours, rustic browns, myriad shades of green, even a thick marmalade-like orange. We climbed through continuous forests where many trees had toppled over, making our trekking almost impossible. We had to climb over a series of thick and wide tree trunks, jump from one down into the dense and bushy vegetation beneath it and then climb up again over the next one. It was very easy to get our feet stuck in a frenzy of broken branches, twigs and creepers.

Trekking on we came across three Dani huts, built totally on their own and a woman came out to look at us, more with curiosity than suspicion. She then decided to ignore us and set about preparing a meal for the six or seven children that dashed in and out to look at us, giggling, chattering excitedly, then running quickly away, before returning to repeat the process. Their meal consisted of just one scrawny chicken and a few bananas and some very odd-looking items which I finally discovered were long, twisted nuts of various kinds. It appeared rather incongruous within the context of the jungle but I offered them some bars of chocolate. This then caused an enormous family discussion as they worked out how to ration each bar amongst themselves. I was very touched to be offered part of the chicken in return but naturally declined as there was so little to share out. I looked into one of the other huts as we passed and inside was a woman with several small pigs poking out from behind her grass skirts, rather like her children. A man, presumably her husband, was sitting in a corner and I could see one hand had lost two of the fingers. This was unusual because normally it was only the women who cut their fingers off. It would have to have been someone very close to him for this to occur. He would probably have hacked the fingers off with a stone axe during his mourning period.

I had regained a trekking rhythm and was able to maintain a steady pace that kept me up with the leading Dani porters. They were always cheerful, no matter what the conditions were and never seemed to tire. When it rained, which was happening more frequently, they would put on huge trench coats that flapped noisily around their heavily muscled bodies, as the wind took hold of the edges of the thick material. We were heading along a large, open plain that had a section of intricate rock formations to the right which seemed to contain a series of caves. I longed to stop and explore but knew there wasn't time. Perhaps I could on the way back. The ground was very marshy and we had to be careful to follow the paths to avoid sinking in too deeply into the mud and covering over our boots. I was regretting having brought only one pair, to economise on weight and space, and envied the others who were able to change each night into clean boots or sandals. I always had to wait for the mud to dry and then try to hack it off or rub the boots into some semblance of cleanliness.

Over to the left there was a large oval-shaped lake which the porters told me is called Hoyoyogu. It stretched out towards another forest and several small hills and there were few signs of life, just the occasional marsh bird swooping in low initially to investigate, then deciding to ignore us. The sky was mostly dull and overcast and the hesitant patches of blue that appeared were quickly swallowed, although they never gave up trying to expand through. We were approaching an imposing rock section within which was set a dark, almost menacing, large cavern which the Danis knew and had obviously used many times. It was here it was planned to make camp for the night. The rest of us chose a flat, grassy area about 10 metres away from the rock cavern. The Danis headed straight into the cavern to put down the baggage and drums of sweet potato and other things and quickly disrobed until their own blackness merged with the cavern's and only their eyes and beaming smiles showed where they were.

Whilst we pitched our tents the Danis lit a fire just inside the entrance to the rock cavern and soon they were unloading sweet potatoes to poke into the flames. They still had so much energy and continued lumbering backwards and forwards with huge bundles of firewood, which they piled on so high the flames were almost licking the black tar on the cave ceiling. In the flickering firelight the rocks on the gorge above took on the weirdest and strangest of shapes and faces, particularly as the remnants of daylight finally fell away. Soon any sight of the valley and the mountains had disappeared completely. Within the cave it was a totally stone-age scene. The Danis sat around the fire, their naked black flesh lit with a reflected glow as were the rocks, their shadowed penis gourds swaying slowly, dappled in dark golds and browns. Part of the floor was buried under several inches of feathers from birds that they must have caught on previous expeditions and which they had plucked and cooked on fires similar to this one. Probably the roof of this cave had been blackened in the same way for tens of thousands of years. Whenever they pushed in more wood or logs or pulled out a potato, flames would suddenly spit upwards and crackle towards the ceiling. One of the climbers was flicking his torchlight around and suddenly he caught a frightened possum in its beam. It had soft black eyes and thick fur bundled up against the cold and it mournfully twitched its whiskers as its body became transfixed by its fear. A shout went up from the Danis as they rushed towards it and I couldn't see what happened after that. I hoped it had escaped but I doubted it. Later I heard further shouts and noises from around their fire and in the cave and then eventually realised that they were singing. The sounds were strange and ancient in their origins and perhaps they too had no idea what they really meant. They were songs that had been passed down from father to son over the Dani generations, from time immemorial.

It was becoming extremely cold and I returned to my tent and huddled within my sleeping and bivi bags, listening to the Danis for perhaps another hour. They abruptly stopped and all was silent and on that instant I must have fallen asleep, as I remembered nothing further until the sounds of next morning's earliest risers woke me. It would be our final day of trekking, during which we planned to reach the valley of the mountains where we would set up our climbing base camp. I was eager to press on, to explore, to see more. There was so much to learn but I knew there was never enough time in one lifetime.

Finally The Danau-Danau Valley

This turned out to be our longest trekking day and I knew towards the end we would be climbing up some very tough rock formations. Today would be bringing us to our chosen and committed destination and I felt relaxed and philosophical at what lay ahead of us at the end. I recalled the gentle but evocative words of Krishnamurti, 'In oneself lies the whole world and if you know how to look and learn, then the door is there and the key is in your hand. Nobody on earth can give you either the key or the door to open, except yourself'.

We were heading to the valley which the Danis call Lembah Danau-danau, Valley of the Lakes, but we referred to it as the Carstensz Valley. I had got up early and in honour of the occasion had shaved and changed socks. It still took a couple of hours to organise breakfast, pack up the tents and for the Danis to load everything up before we could all set off. The sky was clear although there was a long spiral of smoke from the Danis cave fire drifting skywards, all the time creating intricate patterns as if they were sending smoke signals ahead to announce our coming.

We trekked initially over a series of plains, then through a dense, rather forbidding forest, with enormous changes in the vegetation taking place every few metres. Sometimes we were trekking or wading through swamp-laden marshes, searching out the dryer paths but rarely finding them. Near the river sections there were clumps of sago palms, sometimes lining completely along one whole side of a stretch of a river, many of them in flower. Once the sago tree is in bloom the pith of the tree is no longer edible, only the very sweet top of it. I also saw wild jackfruit trees, huge bushes of bamboo, and some extremely bulky and high banyan trees. These were tightly closeted together, their plank-like roots clearly visible above the ground and always emeshed within a grey webbing. The canoe trees and ironwoods soared high above the vegetation, alongside the slender betel-nut trees which curved gently upwards and stretched well above the lower layers of the forest below it. There was also rattan in its many guises, climbing through the branches and over the tops of bushes creating ever more intricate patterns. We even came across a few abandoned gardens of banana trees and taro. They had obviously been planted long ago in rough clearings but then finally left to grow unattended, although one day perhaps the owners intended to return and to harvest the yield. The sun was beating down and I stopped many times to drink. There were all kinds of oriental grasses edging the river and the tiny pools and lakes, bending under the weight of their very feathery blossoms, also many kinds of tree ferns.

A white egret flew out of one of the bushes and took off in a great hurry, flying further upstream to settle down again, only to have to take off once again as we approached and this continued until the egret became bored with this game and finally disappeared from view. I saw a number of other small wading birds and spoonbills and also the occasional cockatoo but they always quickly disappeared out of sight. Only very occasionally would I hear the birds singing, they seemed almost too busy for that. I know that some young birds (the new world flycatchers for instance) learn to sing without ever hearing any birdsong although most of course hear the songs of their adult birds towards the end of their first year. It is always fascinating and extraordinary to remember that birds are only programmed genetically to learn the song of their own species and cannot imitate the song of a different kind; another of Nature's great mysteries, of which as I trekked on there were so many just all around me. At one stage we came across a flock of flying foxes, hanging upside down in the trees sleeping, but they immediately awoke and started flapping their wings on our approach and quickly flew off into the distance. There were convoys of yellow sun birds and the occasional red and blue parrot. There were many kinds of hornbills and these made such a loud noise, beating the air with their huge wings as they soared above, that it gave credence to the old tale that the Portuguese explorers originally had thought they must have been a herd of rhinoceros thudding through the forest to attack them. Within the bushy small-leaf aura trees the glorious fireflies lived and the sight of them always stopped me in my tracks in absolute wonderment at their fragile delicacy.

We met up with several Dani tribesmen, some of whom were carrying heavy bows made out of ironwood and strung with a length of split bamboo, the bows some 2 to 3 metres long. The arrows were tipped with elaborately-carved and strangely-shaped barbs as their deadly points. Some were triple-headed, mostly used for capturing small birds, others had a single bamboo razor-sharp blade for tree marsupials and wild pigs. There were also some arrows that had deeply-hooked barbs. We were told by the Danis they were for 'Manusia', meaning human beings and I couldn't tell whether they were joking or not. The tribesmen were always anxious to obtain cigarettes from us and as we approached they would often chant out in unison repeating again and again the words which I understood meant smoke, 'Isap, Isap, Isap'. It was interesting to watch as with great studied concentration they rolled their tobacco inside the Nipa leaf. Once lit, each would inhale in turn, before passing the cigarette on to the next man. They also often called out to us 'Nder Momo', meaning 'We love you'. It was easier to reply with a smile and a wave.

The bright, clean light of the morning clearly picked out the contours of the mountains we were headed for. They always looked much closer than they really were and even after many hours trekking there was certainly still quite a distance to travel. However we could always see the rock fissures, grey and forbidding, looming high above the forests. Frederick Franck in the Zen of Seeing stated, 'When climbing, mountaineering or just trekking it is essential to accept things as they are and not try to change, criticise or reject. One must see through the eye of the painter. The painter's eye does not judge, moralise, criticise, but accepts whatever is before it and accepts with gratitude. It accepts the long bamboo being long, the golden rod being yellow'.

At one stage we climbed through a rocky valley which led into a dappled woodland covered with all kind of mosses and grasses. We stopped there for a while to eat and we were then joined by a number of Danis. The oldest and presumably most venerable sat cross-legged immediately in front of me. He wore a headband made of blue beads woven together, with a cockerel feather stuck in it and also woven bracelets along his arms. I offered him some fruit and in return, though I didn't understand exactly what he meant, he tried to explain something about the sweet potatoes they were eating and how they grew. I was quickly lost but luckily one of our Indonesian guides helped to translate. It seemed each kind of sweet potato has a different function. One kind is only for old men, another is given to young men, one kind should only be eaten by pregnant women. He produced several from his string bag and offered them to us. They were lumpy and misshapened but it would have been churlish to refuse and surprisingly they were quite tasty.

We were soon climbing through a ring of rocks set high above a gorge. Two small waterfalls had broken free from it and were hurtling down onto the rocky plain below, there joining up with several small rivers all snaking away towards a distant lake. We climbed along the tussocky slope to see how high we could reach. It was a hard haul over the springy vegetation, often needing us to use our knees and elbows to clamber through. We finally cleared the main ridge and found ourselves on a knife-edge one, so narrow we couldn't easily stand up for fear of falling off. We straddled it painfully and pulled ourselves along until we gained the upper barren slope leading to the sheer rock walls. Finally we came to a bare, quite flat, limestone pavement and several sections of crumbling criss-crossed stones. Many of them were embedded with fossils, some 4,000 metres above their proper habitat. They must have been thrust there many hundreds of thousands of years ago at least, possibly in the collision between the Australian and the New Guinean land plates. In the distance at last we could vividly see the pyramidal peak, blue and streaked, capped with snow, of Carstensz Pyramid. We were incredibly eager to reach it but for now it was necessary to be patient.

It was still very slow work lumbering across the next plain, which was mostly covered either with tree ferns or knee-deep mud. We only came to the end of that plain after several hours and then we started to climb a steep mountain slope composed entirely of bogs and burnt bushes. This continued on for a further 300 metres before we had to descend again. The eastward slope of this mountain had been bathed in sunlight, but the western side which we were now on was covered in cloud. The ground fell away below us in sheer sections, sometimes invisible within the white fog. At first the vegetation was in platforms of protruding brambles and branches and we were able to cling onto them as there was no obvious path or flat ground to follow. The landscape then changed again and everything was cushioned in several layers of soft moss. We came onto a woody section, the trees covered with extraordinary large pale leaves, some of the trees bent over and looking somewhat like crouching animals, their major branches much thicker than any arms and they seemed to move menacingly in the mist. At least it was great to be cushioned by the vegetation against any sudden falls. A few fantail wrens occasionally floated towards us out of the mist, to vanish as quickly and I could also hear a few golden-winged birds of paradise buzzing past but they always remained unseen. There was another short climb to accomplish, then a long and rather painful descent which took us out of the moss forest and back onto the rocky trails. Now the mountain slopes became much steeper, eventually becoming sheer razorbacks, on which it was almost impossible to balance. It was certainly rough on our hands and legs and I grazed my skin on several occasions.

A cold drizzle was now blowing into our faces, of course this usually occurred most afternoons, but it certainly felt better than the feverish heat which had previously been beating down on us from earliest morning. The heavy heat is nearly always followed by a monsoon of at least two hours which drenches everyone and everything in sight. Because of the extraordinary changes in weather conditions you would often see a Dani tribesman walking towards you, naked except for his penis gourd, yet wearing gumboots and carrying an umbrella. In our very dishevelled, dirty and torn clothing I wondered who looked the strangest and perhaps who was the stranger. I guessed I really knew the answer but we were welcomed anyhow. 'Wa, Wa, Nder Momo'.

As we continued we often had to cross over a number of very small streams. Although small the waters flowed fiercely and quickly and each crossing we made was difficult in its own way. Sometimes there were logs strategically placed in the middle on which we could balance and use to scramble over. In others there were only oddly-shaped rocks and stones with the water breaking intermittently over them and we tried to jump precariously from one to another. Often we were in danger of overbalancing as the fast-flowing water always swept briskly around our ankles as if deliberately trying to make us lose our footings. Sometimes I did and I would plunge in up to my knees before I managed to scramble to safety. Finally I reached the next long and very tiring slope but at least the weather was not too hot. I was clad just in a T-shirt and shorts only carrying a small back-pack containing my waterproofs and other essentials. I took it slowly as I knew we would be climbing and trekking for many more hours. We eventually reached the very beautiful Lake of Discovery and passed through and over some really gorgeous and vivacious landscapes.

I was feeling much stronger and soon caught up with two of the leading climbers, David Taylor and David Keaton. Keaton had always been helpful to me and he encouraged me throughout the expedition and now suggested I should climb with them. We soon came up to the Japanese woman climber, Yasuko Namba, who had passed me previously, but now I was able to maintain a more steady pace and the three of us always stayed some 30 metres or so ahead of her. I was glad to climb with the Americans as they seemed to know the way as they had attempted, although unfortunately unsuccessfully, Carstensz last year with Hall and two others. Taylor was leading and we eventually came to a very high mountain ridge and there were several ways to go around it, either wending around to the left or right or possibly through a tortuous middle section. Taylor remembered from last time that another of the climbers, Doug Mantle, had trekked and climbed across to the left but then had got lost and therefore he was against going that way. We agreed to follow his suggested route and he led us down and along a steep incline to the right taking us around some overhanging rocks. We had climbed some way down when we heard shouts from behind and turned round to see three climbers higher up, waving and gesticulating and pointing up towards the left, indicating we had in fact taken the wrong route and should return. However Taylor still thought that they would be going a much longer way and we should stick to the route he had chosen. We continued on but very shortly afterwards the path we were following completely disappeared and we were soon lost and presumably we had taken the wrong way. Soon we were confronted with a number of very tough rock sections all of which we had either to climb over or descend back again and try to climb around. Each time we stopped to consider which was the best way or even whether to go completely back to the beginning. Keaton estimated that these rocks were grades 5.4 to 5.8, extremely steep and dangerous, and would normally be climbed with ropes and harnesses which of course we didn't have. We decided to climb on anyhow and would just do the best we could with what we had. There were many scary moments as we scaled across the rock sections, often hanging on grimly as we edged our way precariously across. At one stage we came to a really tiny ledge that we had to cross, so we inched our way along it holding desperately and tightly onto the rock wall, although there was always at least a steep 10 metre drop stretching beneath us. There often seemed no way forward, but equally there was no way back. The minimalist playwright, Samuel Beckett, put it in his way which to me was pure Zen, 'I can't go on, you must go on, I'll go on'.

In descending most of these rock faces there were no real holds and it was always necessary to proceed really cautiously as the way down was very steep and extremely dangerous. It would have taken us hours more if we had turned back now and so we determined to press on. We kept losing the path or a section of it although we tried to follow it closely; at times it was clearly visible but every so often we would again lose it, as it would just disappear and we would have to guess which was the way forward. On one occasion there was a stone buttress jutting out completely in the way and I had to stretch my whole body and hands around it and slowly edge across to safety. Of course by now we knew we had totally missed the correct route and there was no choice but to head down into the valley and climb towards Larson Lake far below us. The lake had been named after an American pilot who, many years previously, had crashed his small aircraft into it. At the very far end of the turquoise lake the trail led directly to the Freeport Mine which we had been severely warned we were forbidden to approach because of its strict government security. After some hours we reached Lake Larson and rested there for a few moments and filled our water bottles from the

gently lapping water. As always only I used any purifying tablets.
The stillness of the lake had a serenity and peacefulness all of its
own. It reflected some of the sky and shapes around it and I
guessed its hidden depths contained its own mysteries. Zen Master
Dogess had explained, 'Enlightenment is like the sun or the moon
reflected on the water. They do not get wet, nor is the water
broken. They can be reflected even in a puddle an inch wide, the
whole sky can be reflected in one dewdrop on the grass'. Taylor
and Yasuko didn't want to wait as I was still taking photographs
and decided to set off up to climb the rocks. Keaton and I wanted
to finish some food first and then we set off after them.

It would be an extremely long and hard trek and climb back
up from the valley floor and we calculated we were at an height
of 3,600 metres. We had to climb and clamber over several ridges
before we could find our way through the Lani Pass. At one
stage we even climbed to a height of over 4,300 metres and must
have climbed over and around these harsh rocks for several miles.
Keaton and I were still a very long way behind the other two
when suddenly we were shaken by hearing an enormous bang. I
thought at first it might just be thunder but Keaton was more
alarmed and thought that it could be a rock fall and as we were
presently trekking under a huge overhang this was worrying.
Then we decided it was probably an explosion from the mine
and both of us felt relieved to realise this. We continued our
trekking, crossing through the New Zealand Pass and finally
reached a section of the original trail which we should have used
at the very beginning. We had taken a long detour and had spent
many extra hours climbing more than the others; I didn't think
it was a waste of time though and I'd thoroughly enjoyed the
challenges we'd had to overcome. We found several back-packs
and bags abandoned along the route by the porters, and Keaton
explained to me that some of the porters were not used to high
altitude climbing and therefore only took their bags as far as
they could climb and then went back and left them to be collected
by those porters who were used to the higher altitudes.

As we climbed the final North Wall, Ripto, our indomitable
Indonesian guide, came down to meet us. He was laughing at
our misadventures and the fact that we had taken the longer route.

He called out, 'Shulman, have you had a nice walk to see all the Irian Jaya scenery ? Why on earth did you take the wrong trail ?' I tried to respond nonchalantly, 'Oh, we wanted to travel our own way and anyhow we were happy to have the extra exercise'. 'In that case,' Ripto smilingly suggested, 'instead of climbing now with me to the right and directly to the camp, why don't you climb further back down over to the far left and take an even longer way around the valley'. Keaton and I both smiled broadly at this but declined to take up his kind offer. As we climbed over the last ridge and finally headed down to the camp it started to rain and there were even hailstones. I stopped to put on my overjacket and hood but left off the overtrousers, as I hoped the rain would wash off some of the mud and dust from my legs. I was now climbing faster than the others and soon left Keaton way behind and in fact caught up with Yasuko again. I had Taylor in my sights as we were both descending towards the base camp but I couldn't quite catch him up, although I nearly did. They had pitched the tents at the foot of Carstensz Pyramid, which from the side our camp was sited looked nothing like a pyramid, more like a series of huge ragged shark's teeth. We huddled together inside the larger cook tent, protected against the rain as it continued to pour down, the hailstones and icy slush smashing hard onto the tent top. It poured non-stop for several hours and I was very happy to be inside. Eventually the remaining porters arrived with the rest of our baggage and we were able to organise some food, mostly cheese, salami and biscuits but especially welcome, loads of hot tea. I eventually found my own tent bag and struggled in the rain to set it up and very kindly the two Japanese climbers came over to help me. I was very pleased to be able to relax inside it at last and also write some more notes. It rained all that evening and throughout the night. We had reached a height of over 4,000 metres and now ahead of us were the giant rock wands of Carstensz. The Danis call them Ndugu-ndugu, 'the high places where the gods dwell'.

Reflection And Solitude

For once there was no necessity to get up early. The four expedition guides were going to explore the various possible routes up Carstensz Pyramid on their own and determine which one we should use. They also planned to attach a number of guide ropes to assist with the jumaring and abseiling as the rest of the team climbed over the next two days. When this plan was announced the previous evening, I had decided to wait until after they returned before explaining that I hadn't any jumaring experience. Unfortunately the mountain practice I had planned in Wales before I left had to been cancelled, as I'd travelled urgently to Los Angeles to assist on a film project. I knew this would cause considerable concern but I was totally prepared to climb a longer route if necessary and make it the harder way. After resting and feeling quite self-indulged for a change I actually got up and dressed around 8.00AM. There were many already up and excitedly they pointed out to me the tiny black dots that represented the four guides as they climbed steadily upwards. It was an inspiring and exhilarating sight as each climber would suddenly spring into view or disappear behind some rock buttress as he continued to progress. The difference in speed, strength and technique between those four who climb all the year round and someone like myself who climbs maybe once every year or so was all too apparent. I learned they'd set off around 6.00AM and of course they were also carrying extensive coils of ropes and mountain tackle to use in setting the rock pitches.

For me this now provided a wonderful opportunity to seek out some personal space and solitude. There is usually always some time for thought and reflection within any expedition and indeed there are many times when you feel very much alone, particularly when deciding whether to continue or not, but it is rare that you have such a lengthy period as almost a whole day to yourself. This was indeed a special and real godsend. Most people spend most of their lives trying to ignore the fact that they are in effect alone; they refuse to recognise that each of us is a solitary person, often needing to rely very much on his or her own personal resources. Although we fill up our time with commitments, obligations, and responsibilities, we often refuse to acknowledge that no one ever absolutely knows what another person is thinking or contemplating, even within the closest of relationships. This inner solitude can sometimes be terrifying and yet, if used properly, can be extraordinarily beneficial and ultimately fulfilling.

Some of the other climbers wanted to play chess, cards or other games but I gently refused all invitations and set off up the stoney slopes of the mountain ridges directly opposite Carstensz. I quickly climbed to a height of approximately 200 metres, where I came to a flat, semi-circular rock firmly embedded into the mountainside and sat down to look around. Way below me I could see a number of the mountaineers strolling backwards and forwards between the various tents, basking in the increasing sunlight, occasionally stopping to drink something or prepare their equipment and gear for the next day. I was the onlooker. But no catcher in the rye. No one glanced up in my direction and they didn't seem to be even aware of me but perhaps they were. I started my Zen breathing exercises and filled my lungs and exhaled in a deep, continuing rhythm. Now never returns. In zazen every breath out is that one, the one now, and it never comes back again. Breathing deeply and thinking deeply are very related. Zen Master Ikkyu, when requested to write a maxim containing the highest wisdom, took his brush and wrote: 'Attention.' 'Is that all?' was the puzzled response. Ikkyu then wrote 'Attention, Attention.' He was again asked, 'Why is that, I don't see any depth in what you have written?' Ikkyu finally wrote, 'Attention, Attention, Attention.' He was then asked, 'What does the word Attention mean?' Ikkyu gently answered, 'Attention means Attention.'

I was really enjoying the cold awareness I was experiencing. Sitting alone on an Irian Jayan mountainside. I had travelled several thousand miles across the world and trekked through some of the most inhospitable jungles and terrain to arrive here. Now I had. These were moments for thought and reflection. I scooped up a handful of small stones and played with them from one hand to another, until they gradually fell through my fingers and roughly regained their positions. I had perhaps moved them a fraction but there was no real effect. The sun was reflecting off the tops of the rocks across the ridges but I couldn't see the peak itself. This was hidden from view and would only be revealed once I had climbed to the summit ridge, assuming I could make that. There is a Zen saying which was so very apposite at that moment: 'Before a person studies Zen, mountains are mountains and waters are waters; after a first glimpse into the truths of Zen, mountains are no longer mountains and waters are not waters; after enlightenment mountains are once again mountains and waters once again waters'.

The mountain's powerful presence was quite awesome and I knew it would push me to the utmost but I was looking forward to the challenge. The American philosopher Henry Thoreau had written, 'You never achieve what you aim for, therefore aim high'. He hadn't been talking about the mountains but he loved Nature in all its forms, knew the need for space, believed in the necessity of solitude and I felt he would have understood my reasons for being here. Thoreau had also expressed, what to me seemed an essential Zen tenet, 'It is as hard to see one's self as to look backwards without turning around'. A mountain is a place where it is necessary to look backwards many times. Some of its rock walls in many places were absolutely sheer, although the rock was pitted and fissured and it appeared to me there were many handholds which could be used. I felt the mountain's brooding presence and knew it was one which would test even the strongest and hardiest of climbers. Four of our present team had not managed to complete the climb a year previously and I knew how important it was to them they would succeed this time. Being here, thinking, meditating, was giving me enormous pleasure and satisfaction and I became fully aware how much I was enjoying the totality of the expedition and I knew to me the mountains were part of it and not the only goal. Krishnamurti in his own simplistic way had expressed what I was experiencing 'Meditation is not a means to an end, it is both the means and the end'. However, as I had learned from past expeditions, I could really understand how someone could love mountains or one particular one and I felt myself completely uplifted by the physicality of Carstensz and its extraordinary majesty.

Many artists have fallen in love with one mountain that came to mean something really special to them. They have tried to paint it again and again, in different lights, from different positions, in all the seasons. Acknowledged as the father of modern painting (although he would have squirmed at that description) Paul Cézanne all his life was enchanted and enthralled by the magnetic force of Mont Sante-Victoire, set within the rolling Provencal countryside, near his French home in Aix-En-Provence, the town where he was born and died. Indeed Mont Sante-Victoire has itself more than once been described as a battered pyramid of rock. If only Cézanne had been able to travel to New Guinea to paint and record on canvas the intensity and imposing life-force of Carstensz Pyramid and its neighbouring mountains. No still photograph can ever capture the inner core and outer power of a great mountain and only a really great painter can portray it in all its exciting and different glories. Cézanne had that supreme ability. Cezanne knew that in order to illustrate Mont Sante-Victoire in its full potential he must include in the paintings the relationship it had to the lake and the trees around it, this balance he created enhanced the strength and grace we perceive in his mountain. He totally understood the overpowering sensations that only a certain light can create and the anxieties suffered by an artist in his repeated efforts to recapture it on canvas. Probably every artist is somewhat dissatisfied with the result he achieves, although to us as onlookers we might only marvel and judge it to be a masterpiece. That was also why sometimes Cézanne left a work unfinished, probably intending to return to it at some future date. For us however it still remains a work giving infinite pleasure and joy, although it is why some paintings are considered unfinished, yet are judged complete. Cézanne, as an artist and as a man, appreciated the absurd and often found and used humour in his work as well as in his ordinary life; you only have to study his self-portraits to realise that and this very human approach endears him to me as a man on that additional level. Just as I know the humour contained within many Zen teachings will always enable an individual to overcome a situation which might otherwise cause defeat. Cézanne allowed the air between objects to be as important as the objects themselves, indeed used it to breathe life into the scene he depicted. His greatest works never sacrificed the important feeling of space and his enormous powers and mastery of colour technique enabled him to describe the nature of form in space with a complexity few had mastered before him. In his 'Notes d'un peintre', Henri Matisse also expressed the importance of the empty spaces around the figures or objects. Paul Klee, another superb and intelligent artist, always stated that part of great art was making the invisible visible. Staring up at Carstensz Pyramid, set within this wild and exotic place, feeling its power calling me to it, I knew exactly what Cézanne, Matisse and Klee had meant. When an artist draws, particularly a great artist, we should always be able to see through the drawing, through the painting, through the landscape itself directly to the artist. Cézanne is said to have inspired Picasso and Braque, leading to their creation of Cubism which pushed back the boundaries of art, probably out of sight, for all artists following after them. Braque loved creating enigmas and hiding cyphers within his works. He said, perhaps more as a challenge than a statement set in stone, 'The only valid thing in art is that which cannot be explained'. I didn't need to give or receive any explanation for being here.

As I stared intently at the mountain, feeling myself being drawn ever closer, it began to shimmer as the sun finally burst through the earlier mists and started to beat fiercely down. The rocks changed colour and became burnished and bronzed. Hakuyushi had stated, 'Zen meditation is nothing special; in general meditation is correct meditation when there is no meditation. Too much meditation is wrong meditation'. It was time for me to return to the now of the mountain. I could see all the four climbers as they were bunched together just below the summit ridge and at first they seemed to be going backwards. I realised in the same instant as the others below did, who shouted it out, that they were in fact descending. In record time they had reached the summit, fixed the necessary ropes and were on their way back to camp. I lost sight of them several times only to see them re-appear and they were obviously climbing down at great speed.

*A proud Dani
father and his son*

The Dani village of Ilaga

A face beyond time

Climbing toward Carstensz Pyramid

Thatched, primitive bee-hive Dani huts

Dani villagers 'captured' on film

*White out on
the summit of
Ngga Pulu*

*The menacing power
of the Carstensz
Pyramid mountain*

The magnificent rainforest, the mountains beckoning us on

A moment for reflection within this great wilderness

Climbing the Carstensz Pyramid summit ridge

*The helicopter ferries in another two team members
to the edge of the jungle*

On Carstensz Pyramid with a view of Ngga Pulu

Dani girl crossing the river

Dani tribesmen in Ilaga village

Everyone else had gathered together in one group to await their return and when I could see it was imminent I climbed down to join them. They were all so very excited and to them this was indeed the climax of the expedition and their reason for being here. I felt fired by their enthusiasms and enjoyed the exhilaration they expressed. When all the four guides had returned they organised a briefing. They explained that, provided the weather held, the conditions were excellent for climbing although we should set off very early and return before the expected afternoon monsoon. Climbing back in the torrential rain would be extremely hazardous. It was time to be open about my position. I took the expedition leader to one side and explained I didn't have experience of jumaring and didn't know how to jumar. He was shocked and even discussed the possibility of my not climbing the next day. However he could see how keen I still was and relented but advised me to take every precaution and to stop if I felt I was finding it too difficult to continue. He explained the principles of jumaring and showed me the process and how to jumar on a rope tied around one of the tents. It didn't seem so difficult and I practised with the jumar clip and found I could manage it fairly easily. Hall emphasised that jumaring on the mountain itself, involving climbing over extreme rock, would be entirely different, but I assured him, perhaps trying to assure myself, that I could cope. The jumar is a metal device clipped to the guide rope and also attached to your harness and the idea is to slide it up as far as possible along the rope and then clip it in to fasten tightly. It will then not undo until you have climbed up to it and unclipped it and so you can continuously repeat the process. If you started to slip backwards the jumar should hold you and prevent your falling. It is particularly useful when there are little or no handholds and nowhere to wedge yourself whilst you try to decide which way next to climb. I was told that there were a number of extreme rock sections on Carstensz where only a jumar would enable me to ascend and although I was somewhat alarmed at this now I couldn't do more than face it when the time came. The Samurai warrior through his daily practice of zazen could still the restless mind and endeavour to achieve the oneness of intuition and action. His committed belief was the necessity to concentrate on each day's task as though a fire were raging in his hair.

The monsoon in fact came much earlier that day and I preferred to stayed inside my tent reading and writing, listening to its overwhelming force as it hammered heavily on the tent top. I thought I could almost hear the sound of a voice, but was it saying, 'Don't go, don't go' or, 'You must, you must'. There wasn't really any choice and I knew I would climb the next morning, but my appetite had vanished and later that evening I had to force myself to eat. When the rain ceased, to quieten my mind, I walked around the camp and watched the water seeping quickly away in all directions, although the creek that ran along the bottom of the mountain remained swollen and I couldn't leap across any more and had to allow one boot to get wet each time I crossed it. In fact at dinner everyone was quite subdued and afterwards most turned in very early, as it was decided we would set off the next morning before 3.00AM, to get back before the expected monsoon. I didn't want to sleep and knew that I wouldn't be able to for some while, so decided to climb up again to my vantage point of earlier that day.

I let the torch's narrow, focused beam dance its way amongst the rocks, leading me forward and upward, until I felt I was high enough and far enough away and could be totally on my own again. I turned round and the camp and tents illuminated by their own lights had minisculed into surreal and rather unreal objects far below. As soon as I turned the torch light off I was swallowed by the blackness and felt and probably was invisible. The air was still and there was no sound initially whatsoever. As my eyes focused within the darkness I began to pick out the shapes of the nearby rocks and boulders and they had a life of their own, as they seemed to move and waver within the shifting but all-consuming night. A slight wind arose and it moaned gently, moving softly and slowly down the valley as if wanting to know who these intruders were and why they were here. It paused momentarily around the tents and then moved on and disappeared and there was silence once again. Zen Master Ryokan once stated, 'At night, deep in the mountains, I sit in meditation. The affairs of men (and women) never reach here; everything is quite and empty. All the incense has been swallowed up by the endless night. My role has become a garment of dew. Suddenly above the highest peak the full moon appears'. I became conscious of my own breathing and the rise and fall of my chest and it was as if I was looking down on myself, although I could see nothing, but I could feel everything. I didn't feel cold or hot, I was just conscious of being one with the stillness, one with the mountain and one with the night. One koan states, 'Hot, cold, it is you who feel them'. I wished I had brought something to read, even though it would have been difficult and perhaps the wanting was better than the having. I stayed like that for a long time and when I stood up I was startled by the loud sounds my movements caused which seemed to ripple in all directions. I turned on the torch and let the beam stream forward into the night, although it only allowed it to exist for a short distance before vanquishing it and surrounding it with impenetrable walls which could not be breached. I focused it again on the ground and followed the light downwards. My boots were causing harsh noises which seemed out of all proportion to the effort I was making and causing unnecessary disturbance to everything around me. It took much longer going down than it had ascending and I tried to quieten my footsteps as I approached the tents, in order not to disturb any of those who were sleeping. I reached the entrance of my own tent and turned to edge in backwards so that I could remove my boots at the open flap and place them in the outer covered section. I took off my jacket and stored it and various other items ready for the morning and crawled into my sleeping bag. Soon I was consumed by waves of sleep that swept over me and I thought I could feel the moment I was submerged and free.

Carstensz Pyramid, The Rock Mountain

I had slept well and woke easily and calmly at around 1.30AM. I rested and relaxed for a short while before getting up and putting on my climbing gear at just after 2.00AM. I could hear some of the others also getting up and so wandered over to the cook tent where Hall and Arnold were already preparing breakfast. It was bitterly cold but I stood outside and in the half light stared up at the menacing, shrouded outlines of Carstensz. It looked formidable and foreboding and obviously would give no quarter. During breakfast Hall told me that he was allocating the main expedition guide to climb with me. I was disappointed at this as I had wanted to climb with him but obviously had to accept his decision. I had seen this guide climbing throughout the expedition but especially over the last two days. He was fast and accomplished and undoubtedly a tremendous climber but I felt instinctively he was not right for me and would have no idea what I was about. Previously he had even expressed his lack of any understanding as to why I should choose to join such a challenging expedition, and he couldn't accept the concept of fundraising for charity as any justification for my taking part. Even now he took me to one side and expressed his bewilderment or was it anger at my being here, 'What on earth are you doing here? Why pit yourself against all these climbers, when you have such little experience yourself? This is a very tough mountain and you obviously don't have the experience and techniques required. You'll be climbing on extreme rock conditions, it doesn't make any sense, I don't see it, I can't see it'. He couldn't or wouldn't see I was not pitting myself against anyone, other than myself, it was a kind of mental challenge. I tried to explain some of my reasons, my charity commitments, my wish to feel Nature at its rawest, to experience its incredible power, that these extreme conditions helped me to become more aware of my inner self and would allow my mind to reach to its own heights. I needn't have bothered, my words had literally fallen on stone, he was totally nonplussed by all this. The explanations, the emotive words I was trying to express, had no relevance of any kind to him. He couldn't and wouldn't relate to my statements on any emotional or spiritual level.

Intuition was not part of his mental make up. He wasn't prepared to listen to any more, my words had no real meaning whatsoever to him and therefore as far as he was concerned they had no meaning. I had met once more, as I had several times in the past, the closed mind. I wondered how he'd ever instructed anyone wanting to learn the techniques of climbing ? Certainly no one like me. Obviously he had never learned and wouldn't understand the first principles of any of the philosophically-based martial arts. In Nam-Pai-Chuan kung fu the sensei stresses the following tenets, 'Teach with passion, learn always, assume nothing'. This was a time and a place when I would have to assume nothing. Anyhow, as a Chinese proverb puts it so succinctly, 'Teachers open the door but you must enter by yourself'. Here I would have to open the door as well.

Initially I felt so devastated, I started to have self doubts. I had travelled halfway around the world to these mountains, to meet at first hand these extraordinary stone-age Dani tribal peoples and yet it seemed I had met up with a man of our times whose own mind was closed and blinkered. He still had his own stone-age mentality. His was a mind seemingly untouched by the teachings of Plato, Confucius, Nietsche, Jung, Russell and if none of their thoughts and ideas had moved or opened his mind I obviously was not going to. I questioned momentarily if he was perhaps right and whether I could or even should continue, but then immediately I knew I had to. I remembered another Nam-Pai-Chuan maxim; 'Strengthen the will'. I wouldn't let his negativity defeat me. There was no way I could allow his doubts and opposition to deflect me from going on. But I felt I needed to create something extra to counterbalance his overt pessimism. In the study of Zen it is important and even necessary to retain a sense of fun and this is often expressed in many of the koans. The sensei will often instruct his students in a way which incorporates his special brand of humour within his own teachings. I decided that what I needed now was a private joke, harmless in itself, but which would help me in dealing with the real challenges that lay ahead. The name of the great Zen Master Kakushin means 'Awake Mind'. He was fierce in his declaration that the mind must be open always. I wondered what was the

Japanese or Sanskrit for 'Closed Mind' but perhaps that was too obtuse and now I just needed something rather uncomplicated.

An idea started to develop itself. I asked if he knew the origin of the word nickname and, after he shook his head, I explained that it came from the 15th Century word nekename, itself mistakenly derived from an earlier word 'an ekename' meaning an additional name. He was obviously still nonplussed by my train of thought but I persevered, 'Have you heard of the Belgian writer Goscinny who created those fabulous stories of the ancient Gauls in 50BC ? Well the Romans, accordingly to Goscinny, conquered the whole of Gaul (France) except for this small village in which lived Asterix, Obelisk and many other wonderful characters he created. Obelisk is almost a giant, immensely strong and always carries with him a huge menhir, a large stone dating from the Neolithic Age. Well you are probably as strong, so I'll think of you as Obelisk', not adding that he would also be my menhir, the very large stone I'd also have to carry up the mountain with me. He just shrugged his shoulders, uncomprehending and responded without the faintest touch of irony, 'It's up to you, I don't care. You are climbing with the most non-philosophical person in the world. I was hired for this expedition as a mountain guide and I've been told to climb with you and that's the only reason I'm here. Let's go, it's time to get moving'. His face was set hard. Lin-Chi's words were right on the button. 'When you meet a master swordsman, show him your sword. When you meet a man who is not a poet, do not show him your poem'.

Our situation was so bizarre I almost laughed out loud. Two men, complete opposites in every way, about to climb Carstensz Pyramid, the highest and toughest mountain in Australasia. Obelisk had immense experience and knew all the climbing techniques, I had little experience and particularly had no knowledge of the technique of jumaring. Using a jumar was obviously of considerable benefit and usually would be of help in climbing faster and with much less effort. In my case it would probably be the opposite as I'd have to try and learn the jumar technique as I climbed. On extreme rock conditions the aim is to climb by leaning outwards from the mountain with only the support of one guide rope, gradually working the feet upwards and then fasten the jumar at the highest point you could reach so that you could not slip backwards. You then needed to slacken the rope ahead so you could slide the jumar up before locking it again into a higher position. Obelisk would always climb ahead of me for possibly 10 metres, then stop and watch me struggle up to where he was and then he'd immediately climb on again. At no time during the entire climb up did he ever congratulate me on what I'd achieved or encourage me to continue and never once asked if I wanted to rest. His face was at all times totally deadpan and expressionless, he was merely there to see that I did not fall or if I did then presumably he'd attempt to help. I supposed I could not really fall because the jumar should be holding me but I did not really know that. I was often using the jumar incorrectly and climbing badly and this was causing me to expend enormous energy just to climb a few metres over the harsh and jagged rocks.

It was now just after 3AM. We had started climbing in pitch darkness, the broken rocks illuminated only by the two single beams from our head torches, but at least I felt I also had a light within. The initial scree slopes were extremely difficult to traverse and I slipped backwards several times. Obelisk of course had no problems with the scree and bounded quickly ahead. I wondered if I was going to be defeated before I'd hardly begun but I determined to persevere. I struggled on grimly and eventually reached Obelisk who immediately asked me if I still wanted to continue. I could really only see his eyes glinting in the darkness, reflecting in the torchlight but I could feel his rejection and it strengthened my resolve. Inside I thought, thanks, but no thanks Obelisk, I'll carry my menhir a while longer. I couldn't help it but laughed out loudly, the sound reverberating around us. My laughter continued to grow and it echoed amongst the rocks probably resounding upwards to reach the others some considerable distance ahead. Obelisk was obviously very irritated, 'What is it, what's the joke ?' There was no way I could or even wanted to explain. Instead I volunteered, 'I just suddenly started thinking about a funny story I've heard. I think it would appeal very much to the Danis. A man is travelling down a country lane when he sees a farmer staggering under the weight of an enormous pig. He then sees the farmer lifting up the pig so it can eat the acorns from an oak tree. Rather amazed he stops and says to the farmer, 'Excuse me interrupting, but if you put the pig down and shake the oak tree, a number of the acorns would fall to the ground and it would save a great deal of time'. The farmer gently replies, 'What's time to a pig?' Obelisk didn't laugh or even react. Even in the half darkness I could see his face hadn't moved a muscle and he just stared blankly back at me for several moments before turning around and climbing speedily upwards. I was still smiling as I climbed more slowly and much less expertly after him.

When we had started out we couldn't know how the weather conditions might turn out later and therefore we had to assume the weather would be volatile and could turn bitterly cold or it would suddenly monsoon. So it was necessary to carry a full back-pack and I had to be fully dressed to cope with possible extreme cold and wind conditions. Due to all the energy I was now expending and with carrying so much weight, soon I was overheating considerably and perspiring heavily. I would have loved to remove some clothing but there didn't seem to be enough time. I was also desperate to drink some water but not once did Obelisk suggest I stop, it was presumably always up to me to shout out when I needed to. With his uncompromising attitude I found this difficult and preferred to keep climbing without asking to take any breaks. Obelisk of course was able to climb higher easily and then he could stop sometimes to drink or wait for me to struggle up to where he was. He was obviously expecting me to give up and admit that the unequal struggle was too much for me and I'd decided to go down. Once the sun started to come through I was beginning to heat up even more. To try and quench my thirst a little all I could do when reaching one of the ice sections was to force my hand into the hard ice and break off small pieces and suck on them. It was not satisfactory but there seemed no other choice. My water bottle was slung across my back-pack and in order to get to it I would have had to stop, unclip the jumar and take off my back-pack and this would have lost more time. Also it would have been a precarious manoeuvre. Every so often, as a release, through clenched teeth I'd quietly shout the Finnish word 'sisu' which means determination, never giving up, and which I've adopted as part of my Zen vocabulary. Once Obelisk dislodged a small stone above me which ricocheted down and struck me painfully on my lip. This time I shouted sisu loudly and he called out to ask what I wanted. I tried to explain but I don't know if he understood and he didn't make any comment. The rocks were becoming more difficult to climb and at times there just did not seem any definite way forward. There were a number of narrow gullies or notches into which I would thrust a foot in order to try to use it as a lever to propel myself upward. This was pretty painful and when it proved impossible I had to scramble myself forward holding tightly to the rope. At times I thought the jumar had broken or stuck as I could not move it forward along the rope. I shouted this out to Obelisk but he always stared impassively down at me as if to say this could not be the case and of course he was always right, eventually somehow I got it to shift upwards. He would never come down to help but always just stood there watching my struggles and waiting for me to make my way up to him or decide to give up. At times my only choice was to crawl on my hands and knees, occasionally practically hanging backwards off the mountain as I edged my feet upwards into extraordinary positions above my head. It was a painful and tortuous process and I was suffering in more ways than I can describe. Each time I slipped backwards and had to summon my innermost energies to try again, Obelisk watched without comment, obviously expecting that this time I would say enough is enough. But I followed the judo dictum of 'Falling seven times, getting up eight'.

5 very long hours after we had set off, I finally climbed to and reached the summit ridge. It was approximately 8.00AM. The height was some 4,825 metres (15,830 feet), higher than Mont Blanc. It was higher than most climbers had reached and I had become part of a very select band of mountaineers who have achieved the summit ridge of Carstensz Pyramid. It was a special and private moment, but there was no flash of enlightenment. As Robert Pirsig astutely stated, 'The only Zen you find on the tops of mountains is the Zen you bring there yourself'. Still it was a moment to savour. It was a moment beyond description,

as this Zen saying quietly expresses, 'Both speech and silence transgress'. The actual summit itself was only approximately 60 metres higher but it was a tortuous route to reach it. It would mean climbing down and across a gully and then jumaring again up to the gully's top and repeating the same across two further gullies. I was very willing to do this but Obelisk said it would take me up to 5 hours to reach the summit this way; then of course it would be possibly up to a further 5 hours to climb back to the summit ridge and another 3 hours to climb down to our camp site. He put it in a very uncompromising way and without providing any encouragement for me to continue. If I'd been on my own or with anyone else I would have gone on but Obelisk was a stone too far and with him alongside me it would be no real gain. I doubted if it was worth it to me in those circumstances. The wind dipped, lessened and itself seemed to hesitate. I stared deeply into the first gully and felt myself glide in and out of the space within. Georges Braque in his works was always seeking a fuller experience of space. He used meditation in his art forms to create scenes which needed to be seen, thought about and their truths discovered. Braques stated 'Life becomes a perpetual revelation, that is true poetry'. The mountain had revealed itself with its own dynamic poetry, did I really need more. I thought about it intensely for some further moments but in the end I could find no pleasure in going on. Modern martial arts such as kendo, judo and aikido relate directly to the marriage of Zen and Bushido, the medieval chivalry code of the Samurai, and are collectively know as Budo. This can translate as the way (do) of war (bu) but the Japanese character "bu" also means to cease the struggle. The emphasis is always on 'do' which also has a deeper meaning of being essentially goalless, there is never a need to be seduced by the necessity of winning. In the spirit of Zen and Budo your everyday activity becomes the contest but there must be awareness at every moment. Without the slightest compassion or emotion coming from Obelisk it would render the joy derived from reaching the summit tasteless and I decided I'd climb back down.

For whatever reason, unexpectedly, Obelisk then said I had climbed splendidly and had reached a magnificent height, particularly without having the necessary techniques and experiences of the other climbers. I had so withdrawn from him by then that his words of praise, if in fact that is what they really were, now had no impact on me. Zen Master Tetsuo always stated that if you wanted to avoid depending on anyone, never let criticisms or praise disturb your heart. Rudyard Kipling in his moving yet oddly disturbing poem, If, expressed something similar with 'If you can meet with Triumph and Disaster and treat those two imposters just the same'. I felt as if I was on the summit ridge completely on my own; I was not here with Obelisk and he was not here with me. I didn't respond to his statement and slowly walked around the summit ridge, taking a number of photographs and enjoying the experiences and sensations of this extraordinary place. One moment the wind swirled and danced around me and I was fully conscious of its strength, the next it had vanished and I could feel the stillness. Emily Brontë's words came easily to my mind, 'When it blows, the mountain wind is boisterous but when it blows not, it simply blows not'. Her classic novel, Wuthering Heights, published 1847, contains as evocative an image of the power of the elements as any great work of literature. A year later aged 30 Emily Bronte died. A Zen koan asks, 'What is the colour of the wind?' Perhaps Bronte had found her answer. My mind was racing and I was in some kind of turmoil as I relived the climb. After a short while I could see 3 other climbers returning just beyond the first gully and they waved to me and were excited to see me on the summit ridge. Their enthusiasm meant a lot to me and was very uplifting. I almost wavered in my resolve and thought of continuing, but decided that I had more to gain personally by deciding not to continue than in needing to go on. I had no need to prove anything to myself or that I could reach the actual summit because now I knew I could.

It was time for me to climb down from the roof of Australasia. Far below I could see the yellow tents of our camp and they also looked like tiny mushrooms, as once previously had the Dani huts; so far away it seemed almost impossible that I had climbed all that distance and to such a great height in 5 hours. Obelisk and I did not speak very much and obviously we both had our own thoughts. We loaded on our back-packs, roped up together and then set off downwards. In some ways this proved more difficult. There were times when I had to climb downwards, facing outwards, cautiously working my feet over the rocks, making certain that I always had something to hold onto in case my feet slipped. At other times I would face the rocks and step downwards, holding on as best I could, as I edged my way over the unrelenting boulders and stones. Sometimes it became necessary to abseil down the mountain face using the ropes that had been fixed into the rocks. My abseiling experience was limited and it was tough and tiring work, particularly trying to abseil over some of the rocks that jutted abruptly out from the mountainside. Occasionally a few loose stones would give way and I'd slip and hang suspended for a moment or two before I could find a foothold again. It was always very important to try and not dislodge any stones, as they quickly gathered force and weight as they fell and could be extremely dangerous to anyone climbing below. Altogether I was still carrying some 15 kg of equipment, including the weight of my helmet, ice axe, overclothes, two water bottles and my back-pack. This heavy load often threatened to overbalance me and pull me downwards and always I had to counter its weight by holding on tightly to the rocks and edging myself gradually and firmly down and around them. I learned that less than 200 people have ever reached the summit ridge and now I could understand why. At times in order to abseil over rock buttresses I had to lean backwards and outwards from the mountain supported only by one single rope, deliberately edging my feet downwards. If any rocks and stones gave way and my feet slipped I started to swing outwards or sideways, struggling desperately to maintain balance and control. The abseil ropes were only fixed in various sections so that we would abseil down that particular section, unhook our safety catches, climb across or down to another section and then lock on and abseil again. There were altogether 10 sections of abseiling to be accomplished and in total I must have abseiled well over 550 metres of rope.

I felt more completely alone on the climb down, carrying only my thoughts for company. They recalled the whole

Carstensz mountain experience and various images kept crowding in on me. We had been lucky to have the fantastic views from the summit ridge; it was unusual to have such a clear day and we could see right down to the Freeport Mine. This mine is the largest in the world, supplying copper, gold and silver and later I found out that 400 tons of slurry each day are piped out to the coastline, there to be picked up by the refining ships. The mine is always under heavy security, day and night, with very tight guarding arrangements, including helicopter surveillance. Permits are needed to visit this area because of this controlled security and are very difficult to obtain. I thought I would like to make my way down to the mine if possible and try to obtain permission to look round.

Previously when climbing up and now in climbing down, my helmet struck against the rocks several times, proving how necessary it was to wear one. On the way down at one time my ice axe became entangled in the rocks and was stuck within a small gully and I had to struggle hard to free it. After that incident I was more careful. It was a long, tiring climb down, with many slips and difficulties as I struggled to find the right footholds. Obelisk would as usual climb ahead of me and I would follow more slowly behind and as soon as I reached him he would immediately race off again. After climbing two-thirds of the way down, Gene Horner, the leader of the other team, climbed up to meet us. He was an extremely experienced climber and knew how tough the climbing difficulties had been and was enthusiastic and extremely encouraging about what I had achieved. I only wished I'd had him leading me.

After a number of hours of further climbing, abseiling and scrambling down over various rock faces, we reached the final stages and could unhook our ropes and proceed down separately. I was pleased to be able to continue on my own, as I so much wanted to be left alone. I could finally relate just to my own decisions. Obelisk went off at his customary fast pace and soon left me far behind. I wanted to be left behind. I worked my way down until I came to the loose scree section which I had disliked so much. It still felt totally unstable and again caused me a great deal of difficulty to cross. At least now I could stop whenever I wanted to, drink some water, take photographs, enjoy the beauty of the mountains and the glorious scenery surrounding us. Here and there were numerous bushes and gorses within the rocks, with occasional blue or yellow flowers. The tents gradually grew much larger and looked quite stunning, grouped as they were in a circle and set within the valley, itself bounded on two sides by towering mountain ranges. I could also see way down the Carstensz Valley and it was an inviting place. I knew I wanted to explore it. I continued my way down gradually, stopping every so often to enjoy this last section of the mountain. I did not feel tired at all and could easily have climbed more and even thought I might still set off in a different direction and climb across some of the smaller ranges. However I decided it would be better to take things easier for the rest of the day and therefore made my way back to my tent in order to change and unwind. I met the climbers who were going to attempt the mountain the next day and discussed my experiences with them, though I kept my personal thoughts to myself. I knew it was preferable if they all made their own decisions and found the mountain in their own ways.

Within a few hours the rest of the climbers had also made their way down, although ranging over a number of times, but all were excited by what the team as a whole had managed to achieve. The weather conditions had been almost perfect, although too hot, which meant that most of the additional clothes and equipment we had carried with us had been superfluous. On the way up they had all stopped to remove items of clothing which so unfortunately I had not been able to do. The four that had attempted last year and had then been unsuccessful were particularly elated finally to have reached the summit. Surprisingly the monsoon came very late that day and was relatively light. I stood outside in it for several minutes and enjoyed feeling its force crescendoing down until I could think and feel nothing else. I was quickly wet through but it was exhilarating. That evening during dinner all of us discussed the challenges of the climb and especially the very beautiful sights from the summit ridge. They expressed some surprise I had stopped at the ridge as they were of the opinion I should have made it to the summit. I didn't elaborate on my reasons why I hadn't. We talked about what everyone intended to do the next day and it was suggested I should go back again with the second team who would be going to climb Carstensz. Everyone else could have a free day and could do anything they wanted, although most of the others decided all they wanted was to rest in their tents and recuperate. One thought he might climb Ngga Pulu on his own and therefore he might set off early. I also wanted very much to spend time on my own, so kept my own counsel as to my own plans and as soon as possible retired to my tent to think and eventually dream about the mountains.

Heading Towards Freeport And My Free Fall

By the time I awoke and dressed most of the second team climbers had already set off up Carstensz Pyramid, just a few were still sorting out their equipment and at least I was able to wish them good luck. I stood for some while watching them making their way, slowly first over the scree slopes and then climbing to the initial rock sections. It seemed it would be another hot day but wisely they had learned from our experience and started off wearing much less than we had. I did not want to remain around the camp for too long and after a lengthy breakfast decided to strike off on my own. As I had thought of doing yesterday, I decided to trek down the Carstensz Valley (Danau-danau) towards the Freeport Mine. I took with me the introduction to James Keith, the Superintendent of the Mine and I hoped he would be able to organise entry for me and a tour of the complex. I told Rob Hall where I was heading and what I intended and he raised no objections to this.

I started out at about 8.00AM and passed initially a series of long, slightly jutting rock faces, known as the 10 witches as they all seem to have similar pointed stone shapes at the top, looking somewhat like witches' hats. The floor of the first valley I crossed was covered with more of the razor-sharp rocks, difficult and dangerous to climb or clamber over, one slip could mean a gashed leg or arm. Someone, for strange reason, perhaps just to puzzle whoever passed that way, had set out some small stones to spell the message or symbols, MU2991. I enjoyed the oddity of it. Because of the heat I was only wearing shorts and a T-shirt and carried a small day-pack to hold food and water and additionally two books and a note pad. To avoid the sharp rocks I decided to climb up over the surrounding peaks to my right; hoping at the same time that this would give some great views and also provide opportunities to see the mountain and the valley from different perspectives. These mountain slopes were not as steep as on Carstensz and I was quite confident of my ability to climb safely. I felt very comfortable and very much wanted to strike out on my own and without having anyone to pressurise me as to the pace I took.

I crossed the Dayak Pass and climbed steadily for more than an hour and steadily worked my way over a number of high ridges. If there were any that appeared particularly dangerous I climbed across to one side and gradually worked my way around them. There were many varieties of bushes, mosses and strangely-shaped prickly plants to touch and examine. The rocks were of infinite shapes and sizes, some pointed and sharp, others very flat in striking, deep-bronzed colours; so many different kinds of environment to consider and enjoy. After I had climbed any ridge I would pause there to look around in all directions, drinking in the magnificent views, then sometimes sit and read from one of my books. Afterwards I'd climb down the other side, balancing easily on the rocks and cross through the wild gorse sections until I reached the next ridge to climb. I repeated this several times and many of the peaks must have been approximately 4,300 metres at their individual summits. There was no danger of getting lost because I could keep the Mining Complex in view in the distance and anyhow I knew where our own camp was sited. At one point I came across a very jagged stone, closely resembling in its shape a charging rhinoceros but it was too heavy to carry with me. I laid it carefully in the centre of a wide, flat rock, hoping I'd be able to find it again on my way back. The gorses and mosses were completely unstable and sometimes I would step on one section only to find my foot plunging immediately through into a deep hole. That was often quite painful and I soon learned to be more cautious and to balance each step more carefully, trying not to put too much weight on any foot until I was certain it was resting on something firm.

The scenery was really exceptional and I felt very much that I was crossing territory where no one had ever been before. This was quite possible as the whole area was uninhabited and very rarely visited, even by climbers. I crossed over a long, mossy hill and at about 100 metres down the other side there was an enormous, ancient cedar, completely on its own, as if some giant hand had plucked it from one of the forests and its companions and planted it there as a punishment. At first glance it being so alone it seemed very lonely, but as I came nearer I could see it had its own splendour and magnificence. It had a very wide circumference and when I reached it I stretched my arms around it but it was too wide for me to touch my hands. It had its own special smell and I could sense its supreme self-confidence. I stroked the rough bark, reaching up to the first leaves, gold-brown, burnt ochre, burgundy and many other gorgeous colours, touching and stroking them and feeling each separate life force. I walked around it several times, looking at it from all directions and seeing it in many different ways. It was a home to moths, bugs, beetles and many other extraordinary creatures of this isolated world. I heard several birds bustling around within its high branches and leaves and was able to catch sight of them as they darted in and out. I was very moved by how fascinating and complex this one tree was. Now I realised it was not and would never be alone, it would always be part of a wider and richer world. As I walked on and left it, I turned around many times to look back at it, and each time it presented another image, another idea and was absolutely spectacular in its many aspects. I could only marvel at what this tree was and what it represented.

On one of the distant, very far-away peaks I thought I saw on a rock ledge something man-made, possibly a satellite or radio dish and wondered whether this had been organised by those working at the mine. I had no idea of its purpose and decided I would climb up when I reached that place and try to find out what it really was. I was absolutely alone, I could do exactly as I liked and it felt wonderful. I was always able to stop whenever I wanted to, rest for a while, read from my books, write a few notes, or do nothing. The sun was becoming hotter all the time so I kept putting sun block on my face and lips to try and protect myself. I was also wearing an old African safari hat and its wide brim shaded me. My hands and legs were being scraped on the rocks and pricked by the gorse bushes but this really didn't matter. It was completely captivating being in this extraordinary area of total peace and beauty. I came across some exquisite, yellow, purple and blue flowers which were grouped in small clumps, almost looking as if they had been specially planted there. There were all kinds of interesting things to find, touch and reflect on.

Abruptly the weather changed. The sun disappeared, the sky darkened and clouds quickly covered most of it. The Hindi proverb seemed likely to be proved, 'When clouds are spread across the sky like partridge feathers, they will not go without shedding rain'. I had been trekking and climbing for over three hours and had covered a considerable distance. However it was much further on to the mine than I had anticipated and it would certainly be several hours before I reached it. Also unfortunately I had not brought my waterproofs and therefore had nothing much to protect myself against the monsoon that now seemed likely to occur early. I was disappointed and frustrated and deliberated for a while over whether to try and go on, even if the rains came, or whether I should decide to return. In the end I realised it would be unfair to the others to continue, as I might get trapped on the mountains or possibly have to stay at the mine complex, even assuming I reached it in time. I was sure I would be admitted as I could explain the purpose of my visit to the mine's managers and felt certain they would let me in. Reluctantly I turned around and started to climb back in the direction of the camp. There were several ways to follow and I tried to work out which would be the fastest and also the least difficult. There seemed to be an easier rock section down below so I climbed steadily towards it and then rested on a ledge overlooking the valley. The rolling, wild countryside, hemmed in by the mountains, made a wonderful sight and there was so much to gaze at I was reluctant to leave but knew I had no choice. I was still not certain however whether to climb further down into the valley itself or continue climbing back over the high ridges.

To one side of me there was a small buttress jutting out of the rocks,it looked as if it had been there for thousands of years and I leaned one hand on it whilst trying to decide which way to proceed. Without any prior indication whatsoever the whole rock buttress suddenly shot out of the mountain. It flashed downwards like a huge javelin, ricocheting as it fell, tumbling over and over again until it landed with a shocking crash on some rocks far below. This obviously all happened within just a few seconds, although the whole incident seemed to occur over a longer period. I was dumbfounded, shocked and then realised of course that I was resting only on air. There was a complete void beneath my hand, nothing to hold on and so I started to tumble down after it towards the rocks. I tried to protect my head with my hands and prevent myself falling but I could see the rocks leaping up at me. I was lucky as I did not fall too far and fortunately I didn't strike my head on anything. My legs were not so lucky. They felt as if they had been cut to pieces and my right leg was pouring with blood where it had taken the main force of some jagged rocks. I felt confused and totally dazed and lay where I fell for several moments until I felt the first stinging drops of rain falling. My Zen hadn't totally saved me, although it had helped, at least in increasing my perception and awareness in trying to lessen the impact. Ironically I recalled the words of Ying-An, 'Zen has nothing to grab on to. When people who study Zen don't see it, that is because they approach too eagerly'. I have often been asked to explain Zen simply whereas of course it takes a whole lifetime to learn and usually that would not be enough. In response I like to quote Louis Armstrong's words, 'If you have to ask what jazz is, you'll never know'. At this moment I wasn't certain what I knew myself, except feeling the intense pain in my legs.

It was necessary to pull myself together and to deal with my wounds quickly. Nietszche's words urgently sounded the alarm bells, 'If you gaze too long into the abyss, the abyss also gazes into you'. There was no one around, no one would find me here and I had no choice but to cope with the situation myself as best I could. A hermit once simply pronounced, 'One who falls on the ground, must get up from the ground'. I pushed myself somewhat unsteadily to my feet and bathed my legs with some water, wiping away most of the blood and hoping that there would be no infection. I had some plasters in my pack and I used them to cover the cuts although they were deep and still bled through. I realised they were not going to stem the blood totally but hopefully would hold temporarily. I now had to get back to the camp as fast as I could, particularly before the monsoon really set in. My right leg particularly was constantly paining and aching and I continued cautiously to climb down through the gorses to the valley still far below me. I thought it would be much easier on my damaged leg if I trekked through that way. It was still only lightly raining but I felt cold and wished I'd brought with me a jersey. It is always said that the monsoon flushes snakes from hidden places and I tried to step warily and avoid the many hidden holes and mostly I did. However once I stepped onto a small, mossy bush which instantly gave way beneath my weight. My left leg plunged deep into a hole and I was soon up to the knee in foul-smelling mud. My right knee twisted around to take the strain and weight and I screamed out as the muscles wrenched. I gently eased my leg out and then lay on the ground for several moments until the pain somewhat subsided and I felt able to continue. After that, even more cautiously, I climbed steadily down to the valley floor. This area was really all one region although divided into a series of separate valleys, each with their different wild vegetation, powerful rocks but glorious and magnificent settings.

It was preferable not to risk my injured leg or take any further chances by climbing any rock sections and so I trekked gradually through the lower part of the valley. One section was particularly difficult and dangerous, as there were huge razor-edged rocks on the valley floor which were difficult to traverse. I balanced myself precariously one to another, edging forward but sometimes having to back-track in order to find an easier way of climbing across. In one crevasse a small, oddly shaped piece of wood caught my attention and I stopped to pull it out. It looked exactly like a snake's head and body, with an exceedingly baleful, single eye peering out of the head, criss-cross markings along the curved body shape that exactly conveyed a moving snake. It was a wonderfully natural work of art and I put it carefully in my pack to carry back with me. I trekked slowly to the top of the next valley section and there was a ridge on which were grouped several huge boulders, each must have weighed several tons. One was shaped rather like a lion's head and someone had obviously helped nature along by carving the markings of the lion's mane on one side. The whole rock had the majesty of a lion and it starred passively but regally over its domain, it probably always would.

It was becoming misty and I was finding it difficult to keep up any regular pace. It was also cold and wet and I was feeling very weary. However it was essential to keep going, otherwise, as it got darker, I could easily get lost and it would be impossible for anyone to find me. I knew, as I had trekked over such a considerable area, climbing so many ridges and then returning along the valley floor, it would not be an easy task searching to find just one person. At last I reached the final part of the main Carstensz Valley and I knew that not too far ahead would be the expedition camp. The mist had closed down even further and the gloomy terrain looked harsh and stark. It was also very wet on the ground and water was seeping through from one of the creeks. After I had been trekking for some while it seemed to me that Carstensz Pyramid was now on my left and that somehow I must have missed the way back and trekked up the other side and across to the right. I decided to continue on this way as it could be a worthwhile route to follow and then at least I should be able to come around the mountain from the top. Also I would be able to see the real shape of the Pyramid as it is normally viewed and reach the camp from higher up the valley. I continued on for a while but it became even more barren and bleak and the terrain became tougher and more difficult. I could not see too far ahead and realised that if I did go on this way I might get totally lost and then certainly no one would have any idea where I might be or in which direction I had headed. There was no choice but to return.

Wearily I turned around and made my way slowly back, losing even more time and feeling very dejected and much weaker. Luckily in the half-light I came across the group of stones which I had seen at the outset and which spelled MU2991. I never found out who had created that sign and what the meaning was but from the bottom of my heart I thanked whoever had put it there. They confirmed that I had been in fact trekking in the right part of the Carstensz Valley all along and that it had not been Carstensz Pyramid on my left and it was still to my right. It had just been a combination of factors, the considerable distance trekked, returning from a different direction, the weather conditions, which had probably confused me. Once more I turned around and headed back up the valley, at least this time knowing now that I was definitely going in the right direction. After some further trekking I finally reached the camp, making my way then immediately to the cook tent where the doctor, Jan Arnold, was helping prepare the dinner. She was shocked at my condition but very pleased to see me. I explained what had happened and she examined my leg, cleaned the blood and mud away and gave her opinion of the various wounds. She was particularly concerned that one was very deep and that if it had reached the bone I would need to take some antibiotics. She thought this could be decided in the morning when she saw how I was after I had rested during the night. She put on clean bandages and plasters, some antiseptic cream and I immediately started to feel better.

Those of the second team who had attempted Carstensz Pyramid had long ago returned and were resting in their tents. The two team leaders decided that any of us who wanted to could also attempt the next day the second highest mountain, Ngga Pulu. I doubted I would as I felt I was not in any sound condition to attempt another mountain climb. It was also a hard glacier climb and would require my using crampons and an ice axe. Only a few of the two teams thought they would want to attempt Ngga Pulu but I said I would think about it and decide in the morning. The expedition leaders said they would be setting off at 5.00AM and that they would leave it up to me and any others whether we would go with them. I was particularly concerned that I might end up climbing again with Obelisk, as I knew I would certainly need some strong motivation to have even a reasonable chance of succeeding. I didn't fall asleep for another hour or so, whilst I debated back and forth the wisdom of climbing tomorrow and when eventually I did I dreamed of meeting strangely-marked snakes and gigantic, growling lions.

Ngga Pulu, The Glacial Mountain

In fact it turned into a long night as I woke intermittently throughout and I did not sleep much. There was an almost unreal silence all around, although I felt very aware of the brooding presence of the mountains. Apart from the pains in my legs, which helped to keep me awake, I kept wondering about whether to attempt Ngga Pulu the next day. I couldn't decide if I even really wanted to, surely I had done more than enough. What would be the point of trying to climb yet another mountain. I had proved to myself all I needed and what would I achieve by climbing once again. I remembered well the Tibetan saying, 'One cannot reach the fifth storey of the Patela (the great building in Lhasa belonging to the Dalai Lama) without starting from the ground floor'. Suddenly full awake, I started to muse on the similarities between the outlook of the Tibetans and the simplistic approach of the Danis. They both had an honesty and directness; undoubtedly two special peoples although totally removed from each other in culture and background, probably knowing nothing of each other's existence I felt they had a common bond of integrity. I was enthused again, my pains were forgotten and it was enough reason to persuade me to go on, I should climb once more. Of course the attempt would be more important than any success. At least I would never then regret that I hadn't made the attempt. It was necessary to test myself again, one last time.

I got up just before 5.00AM and went into the main tent and found Hall, Arnold together with Obelisk and told them I would climb Ngga Pulu with them. They did not try to encourage or dissuade me but accepted it as totally my decision. Hall loaned me the crampons I would need and also an ice axe and the harnesses. Jan Arnold asked how my legs were but when I said I thought they had healed sufficiently she accepted my statement. I was now mentally committed to this final mountain and could only prepare myself to do my best.

After breakfast and gearing up I followed the trail along which the other seven participating members were starting out. This turned out to be a very long and tiring trek up a series of steep and difficult ridges, leading out across the top of our valley. We first had to climb to the summit of Middle Peak (Puncak Tengah), then descend down several, steep, stone pathways to the next valley floor. From there we had to climb up and over a series of smaller peaks until we reached the base section of Ngga Pulu. This was initially composed of huge rocks and boulders. They were absolutely immense and it was with great difficulty I was able to clamber over them. Most of the others had gone on some way ahead and I was soon toiling far behind them. Unfortunately Hall again sent Obelisk to stay back with me, to see if I was able to continue and that I did not have any accident. As previously he offered no advice or encouragement but stood to one side watching my exhausting efforts. At times I needed to scramble over some gigantic boulders or work my way through narrow rock sections cut between them, always not knowing and not being told whether the way I was taking was right or not. Often I chose the wrong route and then had to climb back and start over again. Obelisk was completely silent throughout these endeavours and stood there watching me, waiting for or expecting me to decide to give up. My legs were aching and I had considerable pain in both knees but I was determined I'd keep going. Perhaps Obelisk's silent accusation helped my resolve. At times I had to let myself hang over a massive boulder and then slide down it, without anything to hold on to, until I was able to lodge my feet on some rock projection or ledge and balance myself. There were stone sections with jets of water running over them, down from the mountain and I had to jump across or splash through. It was always a painful process and I made slow, very tiring progress. Sometimes I needed to haul myself up continuous rock sections which seemed to go on for ever. Whenever I thought of giving up and going back always the silent criticism, imagined or otherwise, of Obelisk made me determined to see it through. I couldn't know whether I'd be able to make it to the end or what I might be challenged by further on but I wouldn't want to ask and Obelisk as usual never volunteered.

The daylight had finally broken fully through and I could now see the way clearly ahead. There was no direct sun beating down today and the weather did not look too promising. Eventually the rock sections petered out and we reached the beginning of the ice sheets and the starting point for the Meren Glacier. The others had stopped there to put on their crampons and re-adjust their harnesses and to rope up and I caught up with them. I was still wearing the same pair of boots I'd brought with me, the ones I had used throughout the expedition, for trekking, rock climbing and now would use on the glaciers. They now were very worn and seemed out of place, certainly compared with the very technical boots and other specialised equipment the rest of the expedition had brought with them. As I'd had to borrow every piece of equipment I needed it must have seemed to everyone as if I had come along rather unprepared. I had been given the one type of rather old-fashioned crampon which would fit to my boots and they proved quite tedious and difficult to attach. I was struggling to do this when Hall came over and said he would help me fix them on. Miraculously he told Obelisk to go with the others and that he would climb with me when we had completed the bindings. I could hardly believe it and my heart soared with relief. My spirits were totally uplifted and I felt completely renewed. I could not explain to Hall but he was so entirely different to Obelisk, his warmth, his positive attitude and commitment would encourage me enormously.

Hall and I roped together and we set off up the glacial ridges, he leading and I trekking steadily along behind him. He warned me to step directly in his footsteps as far as possible, as the ice here was extremely dangerous and he was concerned about hidden crevasses which could easily be several hundred feet deep. We eventually completed this ice section and reached another steep and complicated rock area but kept our crampons on whilst we scrambled over it. There were parts composed of extreme rock which were very difficult for me to climb. Fortunately Hall had the patience to wait for me and also guided me on the easiest route to take. He was well over 6 foot in height and of course with this advantage was able to stretch up and climb more easily than myself. Sometimes I had to hang on by my fingertips in order to haul myself up to the next hand-hold. To help me continue I leaned on the Zen saying, 'Catch the vigorous horse of your mind'. After completing that extensive rock section, crossing a number of black ice areas, painfully making further rock scrambles, we eventually arrived at the final glacier. It had now become very misty, the conditions were bleak, there was very little visibility. Every time I stepped into the ice my foot sank right in, often up to the knee, perhaps followed by the other knee, so I was continually fighting to pull my legs out of holes that felt as if they were trying to suck me down. This was always using up valuable energy and it was taking a considerable effort to continue.

All the other climbers were far ahead of us and I was struggling at a rather slow pace to keep going. There were plenty of holes and crevasses to avoid and we had to climb a particularly dangerous ice section which was sapping my energy. The fear of the crevasses lurking underneath also made me proceed extremely cautiously and slowly. The incline had gradually become much steeper and at times I hardly seemed to be making any upward progress. I kept trying to climb as fast as I could but couldn't maintain any kind of real pace. The intensity of the wind was constantly increasing and seemed to be doing its utmost to force me backwards. Despite the pain it caused I couldn't help but marvel at its power. The maxim of those who sail the tall ships is 'Never run from the wind', but I wondered if they'd ever had to face a screeching, scrawling wind on a mountain top. Throughout those last sections the wind was relentless but I refused to run.

Hall was extremely patient with me, encouraging me on and was always prepared to wait for me to catch up with him. What a difference from Obelisk, Hall just exuded positive karma. I never asked to rest but occasionally he would stop to decide which was the best way to follow. The light was fading fast and we were both concerned that there might be a sudden storm or heavy snow fall which might partially block the way ahead. This would make the conditions even more precarious and might force us to abandon the climb. After an exhausting time on this steep section we suddenly saw 3 ghostly figures approaching through the mists. They were the first of the climbers who had already reached the summit of Ngga Pulu and were now on their way down. They were very encouraging and said that it wouldn't take us too long and we might only have to climb for a further half hour. Unfortunately we then kept meeting more climbers returning and each time they would also state we only needed half an hour to reach the summit. I think mostly they were not realising how much faster it was for them coming down than for us climbing up. The way was becoming more and more slippery, the ice softer and more yielding and every footstep was a tremendous struggle. Somehow I managed to keep going and eventually we reached the Summit, 4,865 metres (15,960 ft) at 12.00AM. We had been trekking and climbing for nearly 7 hours. There was practically nil visibility at the top and it was impossible to see any other mountains or indeed any scenery of any kind. I stood silent, lost in thought and time for the briefest of moments. There was sound and no sound, the movement of the wind and snow swirled around me and yet there was utter stillness. The words of Wallace Stevens came swiftly to mind 'Among many snowy mountains the only moving thing was the eye of the blackbird'. Here my eyes moved but couldn't see. Hall and I took a few photographs of each other, grey, almost invisible figures and then he said we must climb down quickly.

In fact, as soon as we started it began snowing heavily and this immediately made it more difficult and dangerous. It was intensely cold and we stopped briefly to put on extra clothing. In these cold conditions it is vital to retain as much heat as possible, as the body's temperature falls, the mind tends to blur and life or death decisions can become unreliable. It always helps to wear as many layers as possible and particularly to keep the head well covered as at least 25% of a person's heat is lost through the head. As he tried to work out which was the correct way down, Hall warned me to stay close as the conditions were becoming more volatile by the moment and proving extremely dangerous. My feet were sinking deeply into the snow and ice and this made it more painful and difficult for me to continue. At one stage I even tried to slide down on my back in order to avoid sinking into the ice. That didn't work out and I quickly struggled to my feet. After each step my boots would bury themselves in the snow which was easily finding its way inside and my feet were becoming absolutely frozen. It was exhausting getting down and my legs were more and more tired. Towards the end we came to a wide and deep, saucer-like crevasse which had now become visible and which we must have passed on the way up. It would have been absolutely deadly if we had tumbled into that and the sight of it emphasised the dangers that were constantly lurking beneath the ice and snow. Eventually we reached the rock sections again but they were now very wet and even more slippery and several times I had to balance gingerly, one hand trying to grip the rock wall, in order not to fall. I scrambled on as best I could, also trying to avoid slipping down between the numerous cracks set between the misshapen lower rocks. Fortunately this frightening section finally ended and much relieved I then trekked down to the adjoining valley where we came across another climbing team camped there to prepare for its own assault on Carstensz Pyramid in a few days time. The way down seemed much longer and more tortuous than the way up and I still had to climb across and over a number of exhausting ridges and peaks. At one point I thought that we must have taken the wrong way to be climbing so many peaks, but Hall assured me that this was definitely the way we had come earlier that morning and that it was only my tiredness that made it seem so much longer.

Eventually we made it back to camp and I changed my pair of very sodden socks to another pair of socks that were only slightly dryer but were just as dirty. I had no other spare clothes with me and I was always changing from one dirty and damp set to another which had dried out a little. The other expedition members who had stayed behind in camp were very pleased to hear about my success and congratulated me, although I explained how much was owed to Hall. I felt completely at peace with myself. The mountains are special places and whether you are climbing on rock or ice there is a closeness, an affinity with the mountain which makes the pain and the exhaustion worthwhile. I sat quietly in my tent for at least an hour, writing the story of the climbs and reliving those moments of delight mingled with the many moments of terror. I had learned so much from all of them.

The Long Return

It was sad to leave this magical valley and these stunning mountains. So many experiences, so much gained but it was now time to go. Also it was going to be a very long trek, involving a number of strenuous rock climbs and it would be an intense and full day. We planned to accomplish in just the one day what it had taken us two days to achieve in getting here. We were aiming to reach the helicopter strip where we had been finally dropped and from where I had set off only to become lost in the jungle. It seemed as if it had happened such a long time ago, since then we had all accomplished so much. After a full breakfast we completed packing up the tents and the rest of our baggage, allocated the loads between the Dani porters and finally set out at around 7.00AM. The only way out of the valley was to climb up a series of ridges which I expected would again test my strength and resolve. I made good time however and sooner than expected I was high up on the first mountain and there were great views in all directions. I turned around, looking back to Carstensz and to the other mountains which I'd climbed on the way towards the Freeport Mine and gazed with some sadness down the valleys. The light was bright and excellent and the air felt crisp and clean. I could feel the powerful pull of this wonderful and exciting region we were leaving, but soon it would be as if we had never been there. Master Mugaku, one of Zen's founders, used this verse to illustrate the impermanence of any lasting effect, 'Bamboo shadows sweep the stairs, yet not a mote of dust is disturbed; moonlight pierces the depths of the pond, leaving no trace in the water'. Nature as always would soon claim everything. We had really only spent a few moments in time here which meant nothing within its long history, except of course to us, to me. I had memories I'd never forget. I felt uplifted by the primitive forces of this remote and spiritually moving land.

I was following close behind four eager climbers who were also making good progress. We stopped on the rim above the large circular Lake Dugundugu, as we met up with a Korean television crew who were making a film about the mountains. They welcomed a chance to hear about some of our experiences and hospitably offered us tea. We didn't remain long though as we needed to keep up our pace and we soon started the long, circuitous descent around the lake to reach a range of mountains on the other side. The water looked particularly inviting but there was no time to stop and bathe. It was a much longer route than it first appeared and soon we were strung out in an untidy line as each of us made our own way around it. The rock face I came to on the far side was exceptionally steep and difficult and at times I couldn't find any hand holds. Of course there was never any choice but to climb on somehow, with at times my needing to jump up and grab hold of a protruding stone, and eventually I struggled my way up to reach the summit ridge. A few of the Dani porters were also climbing back with us, still balancing on their heads the drums and barrels of equipment and food though presumably most were now half-empty. As I descended one steep section I heard a warning shout from above. Quickly I looked up and jumped urgently to one side as a large, blue, metal drum bounced down the rocks, only slightly to my left and just missing me. It continued dramatically on its way, echoing all down the valley and the porter who had dropped it hastily scrambled past me in order to retrieve it. That was certainly pretty alarming and made me proceed from then on even more cautiously. But somehow I had to laugh out loud at the thought that my obituary notice might have stated, instead of perhaps having fallen down a mountain, I had been struck by a passing metal drum. From then on, whenever I saw a porter carrying a drum or indeed anything, as he came closer I always moved quickly to one side and waved him past. When Zen Master Ummmon was about to die he felt he had learned enough to express these definitive statements; 'Cut through all mental entanglements, allow in the universal truth; let go of the body and the mind, shed birth and death; transcend the absolute, establish an individual life; lastly haul rocks and carry earth, to perpetuate the life of wisdom'.

Trekking down into the next valley I came across a skull on top of one of the large rocks lining the trail. Whatever the reason it had been placed there it certainly did not seem to bode well and was presumably meant to be a warning of some kind. Almost immediately it started to rain, the monsoon was really early today, with the cold heavy rain soon turning into large hailstones, beating fiercely down on us. I stopped to cover my head but only put on my overjacket. As always my legs were already so dirty and muddy that the rain should help to clean them. The monsoon without fail had occurred throughout the expedition at least once every day, usually in mid-afternoon and it was the main reason why we always set out very early and hoped to make our next camp before the torrents started to pour down. When the monsoon came it would normally last for several hours and at times it then became almost impossible to continue. There was often real physical pain from the pressure of the rain as it struck the body. Some of the Danis had created individual head covers which they now used as rainhoods. They were made from the pandamus leaves and were woven tightly together. They were so thick and heavy looking that the Danis appeared to be wearing small huts balanced on their heads. We were climbing down a series of steep steps cut into the earth and luckily we had completed most of them before the rain became too violent. The ground was quickly turning into a mud slide and soon we were slipping all over the place as we cautiously tried to pick a safe way down. I held onto whatever was available in order to stop myself falling as it was becoming more and more treacherous. I was very glad I had made an early start as I knew those trekking after me would now find it much harder work and very tough going. Soon I was completely covered all over with mud, my skin and clothes almost indistinguishable. Climbing over the next ridge and then down the other side, a total mud scramble, was even worse. At one stage I slipped and tumbled down the slope through the thorny lianas. Fortunately I managed to wedge myself into an old, split tree in order to prevent myself falling too far. There were several prickly palms around full of leeches and biting ants but I was able to avoid touching them.

One of the Danis helped me to my feet and stayed with me. He was extremely happy and friendly and through him and with one of the Indonesian guides helping to translate, I discovered more about this incredible people. His penis gourd was quite short and curly like a pig's tail. From him I learned that the

Danis aren't interested in or use numbers as we do and use repetition instead. If they want to say twenty pigs they would just repeat the word pig twenty times. This certainly gave a wonderful rhythm to their speech, though extending their conversations considerably and making them rather long-winded, but it was their own way of life and I enjoyed hearing them speak. In each family hut the Danis keep a box of their ancestor 'stones'; sometimes they are the actual bones of their ancestors and sometimes the box holds stones from rivers they believe contain special powers. It seems dead people, as well as living people, are in need of looking after, as the spirits of the dead can become very malevolent and evil and will then try to cause great harm to the village. This Dani was also carrying a long, black bow with several arrows tied together with a thong and for some reason he decided he would demonstrate his skill. He put down his pack, took an arrow with only a single barb and prepared to aim at a bird perched almost invitingly on one of the highest branches of a nearby palm. The symmetry created between the curve of the bow and the bent back of the naked Dani was quite beautiful and I didn't want to disturb him by trying to capture the scene on film. Instead I fixed the memory in my mind and hoped I would be able to recall it as easily at some future moment. The bird itself didn't move, as if knowing it was part of this memorable setting which I felt was in fact being choreographed especially for me. The Dani pulled the rattan cord back so far that for a few moments it created a ninety degree angle within it before he released the arrow, speeding it directly towards the bird. There were actually two separate scenes before they merged; one of the Dani shooting the arrow, the other of the bird totally immobile as if frozen into stillness and calmly awaiting its fate. Fortunately its fate would be decided on another day, as the arrow fractionally missed and sped harmlessly past. The bird fluttered hastily away and vanished from sight. I was pleased at this and the Dani himself seemed sanguine at his miss and certainly showed no expression of disappointment. He just loped away into the trees to retrieve his arrow before returning, happy as always, to load up again. I wished I could tell him something about Zen. Would he have understood Zen Master Bankei's statement, made after deflecting a sword attack by one of his students, 'Your technique is still immature; your mind moved first'. The German writer, Eugene Herrigel wrote it so succinctly 'The archer is basically aiming for himself. Through this perhaps, he will succeed in hitting the target - his essential self'.

It was always difficult to tell the ages of any of the Danis. They appeared to be either quite young, almost child-like or otherwise middle-aged, there seemed to be almost no one of an age in between. In fact many of them I found out were, if any of their calculations and statements were to be believed, extremely young, although always looking twenty years or more older. It made me more aware of the physical harshness of the jungle and mountain lives the Danis live. I hoped that at least the Danis felt young within themselves, even if they looked so much older. Later on one little Dani girl appeared abruptly out of the forest, carrying a string bag fastened to her head which hung down her back. At first I thought it contained sweet potatoes, I saw it jerk suddenly and for a moment wondered whether it was a pig or even a snake but it turned out to be her baby brother. She didn't seem at all concerned about the weight which must have been quite considerable. She stared at us, my Dani friend said something to her at which her face creased into a huge grin and she quickly vanished back among the trees.

We were now plodding ponderously through the forest, which was filled with many different kinds of trees and extraordinary plants. Some of them were carnivorous pitcher plants, always waiting for the unsuspecting insect to land on them. There were enormous stag-horn ferns climbing out of the trunks of many trees. One of the Danis started grabbing handfuls of leaves and flowers and stuffing them in his mouth. Obviously they were edible and he waved to me to do the same but I gently declined. I had already learned that many of the plants were poisonous and I had no idea which were and which were not and I was not prepared to take any kind of chance. There were obviously many things we could learn from these jungles and forests and I hope that some of the plants will one day prove to be useful to medical science and might help in finding cures to some of the diseases which are so prevalent in our own modern society.

On the floor of the jungle if you cared to really study it, and there were moments when I had no choice, you soon realised it was alive with insects of many different kinds and species. There were beetles with horns and tusks, crickets with antennae four times as long as their bodies, praying mantis with long frilly arms, and constantly flying between the trees moths the size of bats. I was standing close to and looking at a strangely-shaped leaf when it moved and I realised it was a giant spiny stick insect, completely covered in thorn-like spikes. They must have been twelve inches long and I backed away hurriedly and moved on.

We now reached a high and sheer rock wall where a rattan creeper dangled enticingly and invitingly from the top. One of the Danis grabbed it and despite his back-pack zoomed up seemingly without effort and gestured for me to follow suit. The creeper didn't look that safe to me and I cast around until I found a pitted but still steep ridge to one side, which I laboriously clambered up, my heart pounding with the effort needed. We then crossed over a section obliterated by some previous landslides of huge rocks that had flattened the forest beneath it and this was also particularly exhausting. We passed a large, rocky outcrop on which there were two rock pythons that seemed to be sleeping, but our approach must have disturbed them because they quickly scuttled away. Somehow I preferred knowing where they were rather than not knowing where they were. A flock of dusty lories were circling overhead and they settled in the trees above us, chattering and trilling all the while. We saw for a brief moment a funnel web spider, about the size of a mouse that quickly disappeared back into its hole in the tree. There were plenty of papaya trees and a few banana trees and I was given some of the fruit. At one time we came across a set of enormous, flowing creepers, that billowed and flowed throughout the trees above our heads, almost in great waves, smothering all but the very tops of the highest bushes and trees.

I was shown what was explained to be a sago garden, but in fact turned out more like a sago forest. Sago comes from the rather unpleasant-looking, spiky palm trees, possibly twenty or thirty feet tall, themselves always overshadowed by the higher forest trees. The tribesmen chop the palm tree down until it is about 1 metre feet off the ground, cut open the bark and inside is this solid, pinkish pith which is the sago that is eaten. You have to break it and mash it up in order to make it into a pulp, adding water, squeezing it and pummelling it until it becomes edible. It certainly takes quite a considerable effort, not like easily prising a sweet potato out of the ground. Until the potato had been introduced sago had been the staple diet of the lowland people of Irian Jaya for many thousands of years. The trees were never actually planted, they just grew wild in the forest. However they always needed other trees high above them, shading them, to prevent them drying out. There is some kind of Dani sago tree ownership arrangement, even though they grow wild and might be twenty miles from the nearest settlement. There is a tremendous respect for those owned by other Danis and no one ever uses their neighbour's trees without permission.

Eventually we reached the jungle areas and we had to fight through all kinds of vegetation, creepers, ferns, wild plants and clamber over protruding roots and fallen trees. There was still thick mud everywhere and often my boots would sink into it so that it covered the tops and reached high up my legs. I could feel the wet mud sticking inside my boots. It felt very unpleasant but I had to ignore it as best I could and continue trekking on. There was always so much to see and observe and the jungle was full of so many varieties of trees and plants that I wished I had more time to study them. Some of the trees were covered all over with creepers and exotic flowers, peculiarly-shaped ferns and bromeliads which took up any bark space that was going spare. Birds would shoot squawking from the trees as we disturbed them. We then climbed down through a section of jungle which grew oddly over mountain walls; creepers trailed over fallen stones, roots hung over the hollows created in the rocks, the forest always pressing in on us from above. There was the throbbing and buzzing of huge numbers of insects.

It had started drizzling again and I could see a few leeches in the muddy pools and they had to be avoided at all costs. There were also acres of pandamus palm with twisting spiky leaves that could flick back and tear open the skin if you weren't very careful. The ground had mostly turned into a swamp of weeds and tanglewood. There were poisonous spikes clinging to our clothes and moths, butterflies and other insects continually fluttered around us. Many became trapped inside the countless spiders' webs which we had to brush aside and which sometimes would become tangled in our hair. We were climbing down the mud slopes when we met up with a rather smartly-dressed middle-aged German team, seven men, seven women, who were climbing up to reach the Carstensz Valley and make their own attempts on the mountains. Each one seemed to have the strong German spirit, although I doubted very much whether most of them would eventually make it to the summit ridge. Subsequently I came across a very tall, handsome, black man called Ozi from a place I think he called Romnia who was supposed to be guiding the German team, although he was trekking a long way behind them. He spoke perfect English though and carried a large bow and quiver of arrows, in order he explained to shoot any birds and small animals they might come across. Throughout this downward section our Danis were whooping, yelling or just screeching in all kinds of strange ways in order to communicate one with another. We also met a number on their way up, carrying the equipment and food for the German team. We were now passing through a forest area without any sign of habitation. There were no paths, no crops, or any regular cuttings to indicate that anyone had ever passed this way before. The occasional palm cockatoo or hornbill would fly suddenly past. I was told that the other major Irian Jayan tribe the Asmats, so very different from the Danis in background, religion and custom, believed that peoples' souls became hornbills for a short time after death, then roamed about the tops of the trees in purgatory, before eventually returning as ghosts to live within their old houses and watch over the new inhabitants. The forest continued low and tangled before stopping abruptly at a swollen stream edge, within a complex of creepers and suckers.

After leaving the forest region I was on my own and I trekked across an open, marshy plain for about an hour. Eventually I caught up with John Regis and Alan Townley from the other team. Townley was looking exhausted and feeling unwell and was making very slow progress and Regis was looking after him.

They were the same two who had helped me when I had been lost and so I decided to stay with them and assist them in return. We trekked silently together for some while and then Regis suddenly volunteered that he thought my team would be leaving earlier than theirs, possibly this afternoon by helicopter. He thought I should rush on and try to get back urgently, otherwise I might miss the flight out. We came to a cascading stream and I waded through while Regis carried Townley across. When I could see they were okay I trekked quickly on and hoped I'd find the trail to the camp. Unfortunately the path I was following abruptly vanished and trying to find the way through I must have turned around as eventually I ended up again by the stream. I couldn't tell if in fact it was the one I'd crossed previously or whether crossing it would be taking me back the wrong way. I know the Chinese proverb states 'You will never descend twice into the same river', but that actually means that nothing stays the same. It certainly looked different. It was wider and the water rushed downstream at a much faster pace. Anyhow I decided to cross it and trekked across the gorse on the other side, but after a while realised that I was getting lost and started calling out. I knew that due to the sound of running water no one was likely to be able to hear my shouts, so I quickly climbed up towards the next ridge. Hurrying too fast I fell down a hidden hole but scrambled out and continued again to climb to the top. I couldn't see any other of the climbers and shouted out as loud as I could, hoping to attract some attention. It was unlikely anyone would hear me if I started to descend so I walked slowly along the ridge, all the time shouting and hoping someone would hear me. Finally I heard a response and turned towards the sound, shouting back as loudly as I could. Amazingly and luckily it was Regis and Townley again who were now on the opposite ridge across from the stream, still making very slow but steady progress.

I scrambled down towards them as fast as I could, not caring how prickly the brambles and gorses were and whether I was being scratched or not. When I reached the stream I didn't bother to look for an easy way across but plunged in up to my knees and waded quickly over to the other side. I continued shouting to maintain contact with them as I climbed back up the slope.

Eventually I reached the place where they were resting and waiting for me and together we trekked on and found the trail leading to the camp. It was only about another half hour before we reached the actual site where most of the others had arrived and were occupied in setting up the tents. I learned that there had been no chance of the helicopter arriving today, as they still hadn't made radio contact with the pilot. Hall told me the radio signals were breaking up, probably because of bad weather and he couldn't be certain if any of his messages were getting through. He intended to keep trying intermittently throughout the night and the next morning if the helicopter then didn't show. We cleared a large space for the helicopter to land and I set up my tent over to the north as the flatter, less stoney areas had already been taken by the others. The Dani porters were taking longer to arrive for a change and this meant we were unable to prepare any dinner, as they were carrying the cooking pots and the remainder of the food.

My clothes were very damp and muddy so I clipped most of them over the tent top, hoping that the wind, although very slight, might help to dry them. Later I decided to leave them out also during the night so that if the wind in the morning became stronger they might dry more quickly. It wouldn't really matter if it rained during the night as they were so wet anyhow. Eventually all the Danis arrived and they looked extremely tired and exhausted. Although they were much stronger than us, perhaps they were not used to trekking for so many hours without longer breaks and rest periods. It must have taken all of us over ten hours to reach the camp site. Still the late dinner, eaten in the open by torchlight, was very welcome. Sadly we all knew it would be the last meal eaten by us in this wilderness, most of us would probably never have the opportunity to return here. I would love so much to come back. The mountains were certainly a major part of it, but the jungles, the forests, the Danis, were equally important. As we ate I could see the moonlight shining on the distant summits of Sunday Peak and Ngga Pulu, reflecting on their glacier peaks and casting a gentle, silvery glow into the night sky. It was an exquisite sight, made more so by the fact I had actually been there.

Living In The Dani Village

It was my most restless night of the expedition. Partly due to the small stones I could feel digging into me through the mat but certainly because I was so very reluctant to leave here. For several hours I lay there in the semi-darkness listening to the night sounds of this incredible country. Sometimes I'd hear one of the Danis shout out followed by some strange response moments later. I was totally awake really early, but I waited until the first fingers of dawn reached to my tent door and, as no-one else seemed keen to get up, I dressed and left my tent to sort out the breakfast dishes. The morning was cold, grey and damp and the Danis were the first others to appear, most now wearing their long trenchcoats or an odd assortment of tattered clothes from those they had been given by some of us or they'd gained from previous expeditions. It was obvious that my clothes were not going to dry out in time and I was happy to give most of mine away rather than carry them back in the condition they were in.

After breakfast, although we had still not heard from the pilot, just in case the helicopter appeared, we all packed up our clothes and equipment into our back-packs and got ourselves dressed and ready to leave. I strolled around the camp taking my last look at the rugged, immensely attractive countryside, already starting to feel withdrawn and distant. I said my personal goodbyes to many of the Danis who had befriended me. The weather stayed cold and misty and it was impossible to see any of the mountains. I was so lucky to have seen them last night, silvery and white-topped, in such a majestic fashion. Of course I knew where they were situated and stared intently in their direction hoping there might be a sudden break in the weather, just for a moment, but there never was. By 9.00AM there had still been no radio contact and the helicopter had not arrived. It was presumed therefore the pilot would not be trying to fly in today and I took my remaining clothes out again from my pack and spread them again over the tent and around on the stones to try and dry them out some more. I was about 20 metres away from my tent when we suddenly heard the sound of the helicopter approaching. There was no time to lose and the expedition leader shouted to me to get over to where it was preparing to land. I raced back to the tent, quickly threw most of the important items into my back-pack, leaving behind many more for the Danis and dashed towards the waiting helicopter. The decision had been made to take the team off first and initially the pilot refused to take my pack on board as he needed to check the total weight. I sat waiting in the front seat whilst he did this, it was okay and luckily those on the ground quickly threw my pack on board, the helicopter lifted off and we were away. Only two of us were the first ones flown out. It was just a 30 minute flight to the Ilaga village over some hilly and forested countryside and I could see several, long Dani huts and other larger buildings as we circled and dipped and came slowly in to land.

We touched down in the centre of the village, in a large fenced field and scores of children and probably many of the villagers came running out to meet us, clambering excitedly on top of the fences to wave. The total population of Ilaga is approximately only a 1,000 people, though many more live outside the village in the surrounding countryside, in their mushroom-shaped huts. The actual village is quite small, with just a few buildings and shops scattered around a few grass fields. After depositing our bags in a secured hut, we visited the shops but they seemed only to have uninteresting, cheap goods imported from other countries. I bought some soft drinks, at least these were bottled in Indonesia. Surprisingly there was an actual tiny bank operating, at which I could change some money and I gave in $20 and received back 84,000 rupiahs. I bought a bead necklace from a young boy, hopping excitedly from one foot to another, for 1,500 rupiahs. There was also a Post Office of sorts and there I bought several air mail envelopes and stamps for 15,000 rupiahs. I insisted on sticking the stamps on myself and writing messages on the backs of the envelopes in the office, before giving them in for posting. I had little confidence that they would ever reach England but most surprisingly they all did. I wandered around inside the village for a while, waving greetings to the Dani men and women, then looked for somewhere to sit down to await the return of the helicopter with more of the expedition's team on board. There was a wooden-framed but covered section with two shaded benches just next to the main field where we had landed. It was some way from the huts and the dining quarters but close to the path used by everyone when entering or leaving the village. Seated there this meant I could see practically everything that was happening and it was a perfect vantage spot. 'When one sits in meditation, one sees the people coming and going over the avenue bridge as trees growing deep in the mountains', Daito Kokushi. Zen master Tenkei subsequently adapted this to become; 'When one sits in meditation, one sees the people coming and going over the avenue bridge just as they are'. Many Dani men and women walked past me many times, always smiling and obviously as curious about me as I was about them. Sometimes they stopped and we tried to communicate with each other. Not very successfully, but all of them always chattering and gesticulating with great humour and tremendous goodwill. What wonderful people they are!

I was intrigued by the different trails and pathways the Danis used in and out of the village and wondered how long they had existed and who had originally created them. There always has to be a first person who decides initially where a trail should be and starts it for others to follow. It can then be used for hundreds of years, perhaps by thousands of people and seems to take on its own meaning and existence. Some trails fall into disuse but normally once one is created it remains for ever. Most trails are made for people to walk along in single file and in a way this symbolises the path most people must follow in life, single, alone even, whether part of a group or team or not. When following a trail you are either leading someone, following someone, or just totally on your own. The Danis walked their trails slowly, confidently, totally unabashed by their nakedness, obviously proud of their quivering penis gourds, knowing, possibly enjoying, how strange that was to us, although by now I had accepted it as quite natural, certainly here in Irian Jaya.

Throughout the day the helicopter kept coming and going, bringing in two team members each time and more equipment and baggage. Gradually most of our expedition group arrived and we started to plan our leaving. We learned there would be a flight taking off in the morning from the Ilaga airstrip, a little way from the village, over on the high plateau. It was agreed that as many of us as possible would try to take that flight. Everything of course depended upon the weight the aircraft could carry and therefore, to get the most people on board, we all agreed to leave our heavy bags and packs behind and just take small personal back-packs. I was the only person who had one back-pack anyhow, but it seemed fair that I should also leave that behind and carry a smaller bag with only the barest essentials I might need to get me back to London.

I spent most of my time either on my own or watching and trying to communicate with the Danis, also buying a few things from them; strands of beads, a large, black, hardwood bow, a collection of arrows and finally a stone axe. I would have liked to have bought more but now I didn't know whether I'd even be able to carry any of these items away with me. I also visited their local school building and it was just a closed room set within a small, circular building, with benches around the walls where the children could sit, although probably they sat mostly on the floor. This room was also used as the communal room or community room for the elders of the village. I visited one of the huts behind the school, where there were a number of women, young girls and small children gathered and I gave them all the remaining bars of chocolate and sweets I still had with me.

I had plenty of time to spare and wanted to explore further. There was a faded, grass pathway leading right through the village and I decided to follow it and headed past various buildings which were paced out alongside. Some were set up as accommodation and communal buildings for visiting Indonesians sent there to assist the Danis and other tribes peoples, or to monitor their activities and those of the foreign visitors and mountaineers like our own group. After continuing along this pathway for a while I entered one of the small, adjacent gardens and walked up its rather tidy path to a smart, white-washed building, and out of curiosity knocked on its door. Surprisingly I found inside some Indonesian travel guides, including Ripto and Rulli and we talked for a while and I explained I was anxious to look around and meet more of the Dani villagers. At first they thought this rather curious, assuming the only reason I had in coming to Irian Jaya was to climb Carstensz Pyramid and Ngga Pulu. Ripto agreed I could explore further on but asked that I should be very careful and not stray off the main pathway, as I might get lost and there was some difficult terrain and dense countryside around it. Additionally none of the Danis I might meet would speak any English and therefore they could not direct me back. I was very happy to wander off on my own but luckily Rulli volunteered to accompany me.

The pathway, which was already starting to break up, soon became quite patchy and indistinct. In the distance we could see the Kelabu mountain. 'Not high enough for you' Rulli laughed, but it looked very inviting to me. We passed a more constructed building which I saw was used and maintained as a local church, probably set up originally by the missionaries who had come to this area. I walked around it trying to find a way in but all the doors were padlocked and any entry was barred. A little further along we found another small building which this time was being used as the local mosque, but similarly this was unoccupied but also locked and secured. Nearby was a further building and Rulli thought possibly it was used by the Danis themselves for their own religious or pagan ceremonies. This too was shuttered and closed. I had learned that the Danis, although not light-fingered in the ordinary sense, often regarded whatever was left around as being available to whoever wanted or needed it at the time. Therefore they would be quite likely to pick up objects that were easily accessible or not secured. We had experienced this previously when leaving items of clothing and equipment outside our tents to dry or to be stored, as sometimes the Danis would take whatever seemed to be freely available. They don't consider this stealing and they have quite a personal code of honour, but anything that was left out was considered to be communal and readily available for anyone's use. In some ways it made a kind of sense, why should a few own so much and the majority have so little, particularly if there seemed to be such a surplus; one of us having perhaps several hats when a Dani might not have any. There were many aspects to this sharing and using other people's objects to consider and I stored away my thoughts and ideas to re-examine at a later time. However I thought I should tell Rulli a story a friend had told me many years ago. She had came home and found a woman picking the flowers from her garden. When my friend admonished her and asked why she was doing it, she replied, 'Flowers are part of Nature, why should you have them all, surely they are to be shared and I should enjoy equal pleasure and benefit from them'. I doubted if I would have thought as quickly of an appropriate answer as my friend did. She firmly responded, 'I agree that would be fair but only if you had also contributed to the planting and looking after the flowers. If you had done some of the work I would be happy to share the flowers with you, but this isn't the case and therefore would you please leave the flowers only for me'. Rulli laughed at the story but I wasn't certain if he really understood it or agreed with it.

We found a new, narrow trail and followed it for some way, continuing past two very ramshackled buildings, the path often blocked with mottled, greying logs, rotting twigs and foliage, with dark sticky mud on either side of the path we needed to avoid. In front of us were huge, over-blown trees rising from behind translucent spear-high grasses. We arrived at one, small, quite solitary house, built on top of thin but sturdy poles and reached only by a ladder of sticks tied together with rattan grasses. It was some 5 metres above the ground. Beside the ladder was a small pool of water where you were meant to wash your feet before climbing into the house itself. The rungs were unevenly spaced and very far apart which made them difficult to climb, although I saw two young children and even a woman carrying firewood and other items on her back mount the steps with ease. Across some fields in the distance I could see a group of Danis moving slowly towards us and I wanted to meet up with them. We walked to the cross path so they could not pass without my being able to greet them. There were about ten of them, all were female, a few very young girls. They wore grass skirts with beads and necklaces hanging down over their bare, dark-brown bodies. They probably did not intend to stop but I spoke to them, although I knew they could not understand what I had said and politely they paused. I gestured towards the brightly-coloured rows of beads that one girl was wearing and tried to indicate that I wished to purchase them. They all started chattering incessantly, obviously trying to decide what I meant and wanted. At last she seemed to understand and took off one row of beads and held them out to me. I shook my head and reached out to indicate the other rows of beads but she shrunk away from my hand. The rest were all still smiling and chattering excitedly, except for this one who had a rather wary look, not knowing exactly what I wanted. Rulli tried to explain I was interested in buying all the beads and eventually she understood. She shook her head as if I had asked for something totally improper and put back on the single strand that she had offered me previously. I was standing very close to her and I touched and held all the strands and withdrew some money from my bag and offered it to her in exchange. She was obviously tempted but still she shook her head. The others were more impressed and were obviously trying to insist that she make the sale to me. By the way she was behaving I started to realise that she would be embarrassed in having to take off all her beads, as if in doing so she would become too naked. I persisted and only after a great deal of haggling and discussion, with great laughter from her friends, did she finally agree. When she had taken off all her beads and I had given her the money, she kept covering up her body with her hands as if trying to avoid letting everyone see that she was wearing no coverings of any kind. The beads really covered very little but presumably they were symbolic to her as some kind of clothing. Much later on the way back to the village I saw her again and by then she had acquired a sleeveless shirt which she was wearing perhaps in order to avoid, at least to herself, appearing naked until she could put on some more beads. With or without the beads she still was full of charm and beauty and was very much a credit to the village. The greatest Haiku poet Basho once met a pretty, demure peasant girl and quietly and simply stated, 'This year I have seen something better than flowers'. Now I had.

One of the other women in the group had wide, round eyes, her beautifully full cheeks set in an almost perfectly-circular face. However her head had been totally shaved and Rulli found out that this was as a mark of respect for her brother who had recently died. She had mourning strings hanging from her neck, covering part of her chest and back and also wore an ill-fitting cap of interwoven sago leaves folded so that her face could be partly hidden, particularly outside her own home. Additionally tufted bands of twisted fibre had been woven around her upper arms and wrists and even her upper thighs just above the knees and down as far down as her calfs. These special signs of mourning were worn until they disintegrated by themselves, perhaps months later. Her small skirt seemed to be just a wide grass belt around her waist to which were tied strips of sago leaf, bunched together between her legs and tied up at the back. She had a number of cassowary quills stuck vertically through her nostrils as decorations. I was told that some women in mourning for lost relatives smear their faces all over with yellow clay. Another woman, although presumably not in mourning, was also decorated with cassowary quills through her nostrils, these quills much longer than the others. She had mother-of-pearl segments strung together in a necklace around her neck. Beneath that, another necklace composed of parts of jaw bones which I learned were actually human bones and they were also tied to two, long cassowary quills. The jaw bones were meant to be from the heads of enemies of their tribe but we couldn't find out how they were acquired. Possibly they had been handed down from one generation to another, although of course they might have been acquired more recently in ways which if so were better left unknown.

Three Dani men came up to us, curious and inquisitive and were happy to join in our conversations. I was told that most of the tribesmen had at least two wives and when I asked one who was the most beautiful, with Rulli translating, he declared the one who cooked the best of course. All the women laughed at this. Another common practice was for a man to marry two or more sisters from the same family. We were now all getting on so well that we were invited to walk with the men and visit their huts. I was thrilled at this and very eager to learn as much as possible from them.

Inside one hut we were shown some intricately carved drums. They were patinated to a deep, shiny black, by the countless hands that had rubbed, caressed or struck them over many years. These and all the other drums were always given their own names, usually the names of elders or relatives who had been killed in battles or had died early. I learned that they believed that death only came about through magic, usually through the hand of an enemy, except those deaths of the very young or the very old. It was always necessary to avenge a death. They explained that the spirits of the dead people demanded vengeance before they could then leave the land and those still living, for a place which was sometimes known as Safan, the so-called land of the dead. Most artifacts, shields and other objects are carved and named to remind the living of their obligations to those that have died, particularly in battle and defending their homes. The tribesmen like to chew spiced, pressed tobacco and it was obvious many have become totally addicted to this. The Danis sat themselves in a circle within the one room, in the centre of which, near the fire, was a small mound of tobacco. The younger men rolled the tobacco inside nipah leaves, whilst the older ones filled their decorated bamboo pipes. One of the Danis picked up a small stick of firewood with its end glowing red hot and from it, passing from one hand to another, each person lit his own tobacco. I refused the offer to indulge but Rulli accepted. They all inhaled deeply, each time expelling the smoke with a loud sign as if in deep satisfaction.

Rulli told me that when the monsoon rains came, which could be every day, the water would pour through the holes in the roof. They would then adjust the roof leaves to block up the leak but the rain would then usually come through somewhere else. An elderly Dani explained to us how important it was for everyone to work together as a team, as tribesmen, as villagers, rather than thinking of themselves as individuals and not caring about any others. He said 'We should all think of ourselves as sticks. You see, if you take one stick,' and he pulled out a stick from a pile, 'It's weak and easy to break,' and he snapped it quickly in half. 'But if you take a bundle of sticks and tie them together with rattan, then you will see how difficult it is to break them. That is why we must always remain together'. To emphasise his point he tapped his penis gourd several times. It was long and pointed like a unicorn, topped off with cuscus fur that made it look like an overlarge pipe cleaner. He offered me something to drink out of a battered bamboo container. I was reluctant but he pressed me and I didn't want to refuse him. It was quite sweet and pleasant and at my surprised reaction he shouted out, 'wa, wa, wa' and tapped his gourd again in appreciation.

Later, in another larger hut I was introduced to a group of men who were working on designing one of their war shields. They sat close together on one side of the Jeu, next to the doorway to obtain as much light as possible. Six or seven men held a shield across their laps, as each one of them defined the relief on part of the surface with a small nail chisel. I was told that if a shield feast is to take place then the better carvers of the village are asked to make shields by those villagers who want memorials to commemorate recently dead or even long dead relatives. The carvers trek deep into the jungle to bring back the buttress roots of the mangrove tree. At feast times they go also into the jungle and cut down hundreds of sago trees in order to find the grubs of the capricorn beetles that then mature six or seven weeks later, after being placed in holes in cut tree trunks. In these holes the beetles lay their eggs producing the larvae, which are then eaten raw or roasted over the hot coals. As soon as it becomes dark the carvers stop work and cover the shields with sago leaves to prevent any of the spirits deserting them before they have been properly named. Some return home to be with their families but most want to remain within the Jeu, in order to stay close to the shields and the spirits they now contain. After eating their morning sago the carvers begin again and as shields are completed they bring in carved wooden bowls of different powdered pigments; white lime made from burnt, crushed mussel shells, red ochre, black soot from the fire. These are the three basic colours. The pigments are mixed with water and worked in with a thin stick or with the finger. Initially white is placed over most of the shield, red then being painted on the inside and the outlines of high relief, with finally the black being rubbed into the raised outline of each design itself. This is carried out by the men as it is usually considered too important work for women. They help by preparing decorative tassels, usually by rolling sago fronds into thread over their own heels or thighs, then tying the threads into small holes cut along the side of the shields and around the phallic projections.

When too many ghosts and spirits have returned to a village and it is becoming crowded out then they have to be persuaded to leave. This is usually organised by planning a great feast. The master carver of the village makes an ancestor pole carved from a large buttress-rooted tree, which is cut and whittled over a lengthy period until it becomes the great totem. It will represent all the men who have died over recent years, the least important at the bottom, the great warlords at the top. Included on it are the motifs of revenge, as all death is considered unnatural and must be avenged. The top figure is usually given a large and intricately carved phallus and the bottom section is fixed across a small canoe.

The tribesmen have many different status symbols and I was able to find out about a few. If a man has a small feathered bag hanging at his chest, rather than across his back, this means he is considered to be extremely important in the village. Again, the number of pig tusks he has tied around him also shows his importance, previously these were used to indicate the number of enemies he had killed in battle. Another symbol relates to the tassels of sago fronds tied in their hair. The symbols on the shields are simplistic, but every single cut and notch and even their length has a special meaning and can be understood by the other members of their tribes, but additionally by their enemies. Some designs contain great powers and a spirit that can frighten an enemy to death. Once he recognises this symbol he should drop his weapons and run away in terror. When a shield has been named after an ancestor and the ceremony followed, then that shield also contains the powers and spirit of the ancestor and enables the living relative using the shield to have supreme fearlessness and courage in the face of all odds. He should be able to overpower his enemy and become the victor in any battle. I didn't ask what happened if he should meet an enemy with greater powers in his shield, whose ancestors were stronger and mightier and therefore more capable of winning the battle. Anyhow I understood these battles no longer took place, except on a ceremonial basis, or if they did it was certainly a secret the tribesmen kept to themselves. I was told that great carvers are few and far between and are much sought after. When a tribesman needs a shield carved then he has to find the best carver he can and take on the responsibility of feeding the carver and his family whilst the shield is carved. This might take weeks or even months. The work is always carried out with great ceremony and enormous respect as it is summons up the spirits of the dead ancestor.

I was really intrigued to hear about the custom of papisj, wife exchange, which was often carried out between the Dani tribesmen. This was usually accompanied by one Dani passing over some valued object such as a spear or even a pig. It depended on which female he thought most interesting or attractive. It is not only physical attraction that would most appeal, but there are other personal attributes that are more meaningful to the individual Dani. Sometimes wives are only exchanged on ritual occasions and for short periods of time or perhaps when someone is under great stress or when there is talk of rebellion or warfare. Very close friends are always willing to exchange wives as a sign of their friendship.

One of the greatest forces within the tribal customs is connected to the power of the snake. I learned the story of the giant snake that occasionally crawls through the villages, sniffing and smelling the feet of the inhabitants and deciding if they deserve to live or should be swallowed whole. The villagers tell the story of the snake to their children in order to frighten them into behaving themselves. The Danis love to tell stories and usually they always begin with the words "Tare Atakam" meaning "In olden times". The names they give to the people in the stories are exceptionally descriptive and reflect the lack of shyness they have about the human body and its parts. In one story the man is called Sosoktsjemen meaning Black Penis and the woman is called Tsjenakat meaning Good Vagina. The Creator of the World is known as Fumeripitsj.

I could have stayed with these wonderfully friendly and warm people for many more hours, but Rulli warned me it was getting late and I knew it was necessary to return and find out what was happening with the others. The Danis were reluctant to let me go and offered me more food, drinks and presents. I refused, they had given me so much, but I warmly passed to them some small personal items which they received with tremendous glee, making loud clucking noises which I took to be in appreciation. We tapped each others arms, shoulders and chests and I was so sad to leave them. They came out to wave us off and each time I turned around they were still waving. Then they were gone. Rulli and I walked quickly through the village. We passed several groups of young women and girls and they all seemed to be laughing and happy. In the main hut I found that most of our team had been flown in and dinner was about to be served. The food was plentiful and varied and the best I'd had since starting out on this thrilling expedition. However I was still very fired up by my special and interesting times earlier with the Danis.

We worked out who would be leaving on the flight out in the morning and it was agreed the basis should be first in, first out. As I had taken the first flight into Ilaga it meant I was counted in. It unfortunately meant that those who had only just arrived might be left behind and would have to wait for the following day's flight, but there had to be some system and not everyone could go. At least I would be leaving my back-pack behind and travelling in just the clothes I stood up in, with only a few personal items, although still hoping I'd be allowed to take my newly-acquired bow and collection of arrows. That night if we wanted, we were given the opportunity to sleep inside a larger hut, two adjoining rooms with very basic facilities, in which there were two, long communal beds. I was pleased to do this and laid out my sleeping bag alongside one of the walls. A few of the team preferred to put up tents and sleep outside, but there were plenty of mosquitos buzzing around and I thought it too risky and preferred the bed. In the morning those in the tents had been bitten incessantly throughout the night so I knew my decision had been the right one. Even inside the hut I covered myself liberally with mosquito repellent and sprayed it all around my sleeping bag. I'd rather put up with the smell than take the risk of mosquito bites and most of my companions did the same. We turned in shortly after dinner. So much had occurred during the day and in my meetings with the Danis that I needed to think about, I found it difficult to sleep, although I tried not to disturb the four others tucked tightly alongside me. As the strange noises of the night quietened around me, the sounds made by the few mosquitos inside seemed to increase. I clutched my mosquito spray and every time I awoke I sprayed some more and hoped it would have the desired effect. I guess I was lucky again.

Nabire, Biak, Singapore, London

I woke up and got up early at 5.00AM and enjoyed a filling breakfast of soup, rice, lots of bread and heaps of coffee. It was time to go. Then there was a tiring, one hour walk, mostly uphill to the airstrip. In order to carry everything I could with me I was wearing my mountain jacket, the pockets again packed full. It was extremely hot and I was soon sweating profusely. We crossed a rickety, wooden bridge built precariously over a coursing mountain stream that raced down one side of the hill shooting spray in all directions. It was yet another wonderful memory to take back with me of this exciting, remote world. The rich vast diversity of human life which can be found and experienced in every part of this amazing planet is sometimes too much to comprehend. 'The mystical is not How the world is, but That it is', Ludwig Wittgenstein. I was also carrying the bow and arrows, although everyone assured me that there would be little chance of my getting them on the plane, but I could but try. Eventually the path reached the plateau and as soon as I arrived at the airstrip I quickly stripped off most of my clothes in an effort to cool down.

I stayed with the Danis, knowing that these would be the last times I would spend with them. Other Danis continued to arrive at the airstrip from all directions, many out of curiosity and interest, but some of them also wanted to say goodbye to us. Two further climbers had come along on the off-chance that they would be taken on board as well. To the side of the airstrip was a very old-fashioned weighing machine, being used to calculate the weight of the individuals and the luggage. It was a totally unsophisticated system. In fact no one asked to weigh my bow, nor my heavy jacket containing my cameras and other items. Finally it was agreed the aircraft would take all the eleven mountaineers present and all the luggage, they would even probably have taken another person as well. Fortunately it meant I could also take with me the bow and arrows and I was absolutely delighted. I rushed quickly around, shaking hands for the last time with all the Danis I knew and many others as well. Some honoured me by giving their special greeting of crooking two fingers of their right hands to lock into two fingers of mine, and then enthusiastically wagging our fingers up and down. We also tapped each other on the arms and shoulders as a way of expressing friendship and saying a very sad goodbye. One or two even tapped their penis gourds causing them to quiver and this made us all laugh out loud. It was a good way to leave these brave, strong and straight-forward people. On board I craned my neck to watch them from the window, a final glimpse as they waved up at us and then they instantly and sadly vanished from sight.

The flight to Nabire took us just over one hour and, after arriving, there was then a very short stop-over before the subsequent flight took off to the island of Biak at midday. We purchased some soft drinks and I tried to rearrange my hand luggage as best I could. On the flight I was seated next to a prosperous Indonesian rice merchant who was keen to tell me something about the island. From him I learned that Biak is the best known of the former Schouten Islands and the most populated. The islanders are Melanesians, culturally very different from the mainland Irianese. I also read that Biak covers 1,834 sq. kilometres and the northernmost shore reaches within 60 kilometres of the equator and the middle of the island lies at 1 degree south. The island is composed of coral limestone with some of the richest and most unspoilt reefs. The constant heavy rainfall has eroded the soft limestone cliffs into innumerable caves and these were used extensively by the Japanese soldiers during World War II.

As soon as we landed at Biak airport, we all rushed over to the offices of Garuda Airlines in order to try and change our flight tickets and make use of the extra day we had gained. After some lengthy explanations and several faxes eventually I was able to arrange an earlier flight back and I felt pleased there was no real necessity to wait around in Biak. My flight out was re-scheduled for the next morning. We took a taxi to the Airport Beach Hotel which, although it had rather poor facilities by normal standards, seemed to me very acceptable after the very tough conditions we had been experiencing. I checked quickly into my room but found there was no running water from the taps and it had no telephone. Eventually I was able to arrange for the water to be turned on and I shaved and showered, taking as much time as I wanted. I tried to make contact with my Indonesian Red Cross colleague, Joen Diaz, but again had no luck getting through.

Wanting to make the most of my time I took a group taxi down town to try and buy some fresh clothes. The taxi driver had a fare collector with him who bartered with me on the cost of the ride. He agreed to take me to the Telecom Building where there were facilities for sending faxes and making international telephone calls. I tried to get through to London directly but without any success and eventually used an operator to accomplish this. My family were pleased to learn I was safe and hear a few of my adventures. I also tried to send a fax through to my London office but this wasn't possible. Afterwards I walked along the main road into the town to explore the shops and buy some clothes. I was able to purchase a pair of trousers, a T-shirt, underwear and some pairs of socks. I also tried to buy sandals but all of them were too small; the Indonesian people, like the Philipinos, are usually built quite small and the largest sandals or shoes in the shop were still too small for me. This meant I would continue to wear all the way back to London the same boots that I had worn travelling to Indonesia and throughout the expedition. Perhaps by now I should consider them my lucky boots. I changed in the shop into the new clothes, and happily threw away my old ones. The shopkeeper was extremely welcoming and hospitable to me and gave me something to drink and a variety of biscuits. She and her colleagues were obviously very curious about me and using the very limited English at their command tried to ask me as many questions as they could. I felt very comfortable with them and enjoyed being with them.

Feeling almost a new man, I decided to window-shop past the other shops and the restaurants and explore the down-town area. This proved to be not too wise a decision. The pavements there were more or less unmade and as dusk approached everything was shrouded in darkness, as most of the shops had extremely sparse and poor lighting. I was approached a number of times by different people who wanted to speak to me or make contact for whatever reason and I clutched my bag containing my passport and money closer to me, realising how somewhat unprotected I was. I found a small but clean restaurant and entered to order something to eat. There was no menu and the waiters only spoke Indonesian but after a great deal of sign language they brought me a steaming bowl full of rather odd things but which tasted delicious. Afterwards I tried to stop a taxi to get back to the hotel but none would and I was not certain how the system worked and couldn't find a single, empty taxi. Eventually I managed to find one of the group taxis and, as the driver didn't speak English, asked again for the Telecom Building, as at least I knew where that was and it seemed a good point of contact. Again I had to barter and negotiate the fare. At the Telecom Building I tried to send some faxes to London but still had no success. I asked how long it would take to walk back to the Airport Beach Hotel and was told it would be just a few minutes. It had become quite dark and I was most concerned about being bitten by mosquitos but anyhow walked for some way and hoped that I was heading in the right direction. After several hundred metres I stopped at a house set back from the roadside, and asked my way again and was told that it was only a minute to the hotel. However I had to walk for about 25 minutes in the very oppressive heat and humidity and I was soon perspiring but eventually I reached the hotel.

Previously I had been invited to dine by a few of the other climbers. They were staying at a larger hotel where perhaps sensibly they had booked in, but I had preferred to remain on my own, on this very last night and to enjoy the local sights, the town's smells and to experience the Biak night. I was still hungry however and decided to eat something in the hotel restaurant. The three Japanese climbers, Yasuko Namba, Koichi Ono, Yukimitsu Okubo, were also eating there and I was asked to join them. My food was initially served up cold but I was wary of this and insisted that they heat the soup and the rice. We got into conversation with an excitable Indo-Chinese and he told us about his life in Indonesia and his problems about not being accepted by either the Indonesian or the Chinese communities; he was good to talk to, knowledgeable and very interesting. Later, after sharing a final coffee, I said goodbye to my Japanese climbing companions and returned to my hotel room to enjoy the considerable luxury of sleeping in cotton sheets on what seemed an incredibly soft mattress.

My flight out from Biak airport was at 11.15 AM, so there was need to rush in the morning but I was used to getting up early and it proved impossible to lie in bed later than 8.00AM. Still it meant I could shave again and luxuriate in a leisurely shower, although perhaps that is not quite the way to describe it. There was hot water coming through the taps in the basin in the bedroom but no hot water system in the shower room. Just a large tank of cold water and a ladle to splash the water over your body as you stood in a draining floor trough. It still felt great though and I took my time emptying most of the tank, before drying off with two handkerchief-sized towels the hotel had provided. Breakfast was served outside on an open veranda and I wanted to be ready to leave the hotel at 9.30AM. I met up with a few other climbers also breakfasting, they having later flights than me and we said our goodbyes once again. The oldest of the climbers and one of the nicest amongst the team, was Reinhold Ullrich from California. He showed me a Japanese sword he had purchased the night before and asked me if I thought it was old. I doubted it but decided not to venture an opinion as it was something he'd already purchased. I suggested naively on purpose he should ask one of the Japanese climbers. I waved goodbye to him and lifted my bow and arrows in friendship as I set off and he waved his sword back. Weapons from two very different cultures and many centuries apart.

I walked across to the airport, only about 200 metres away and checked myself in. At first the customs officer looked askance at the bow and arrows, but after a long discussion agreed I could take them on board provided I paid to have them wrapped and packaged securely. I was happy to do this as it made them easier to carry. The flight for a welcome change left exactly on time and the first stop was Ujung Pandang again. One hour later we took off again and the next destination was Jakarta and from there I was re-routed through Singapore (flying on the beautifully named Silk Air) to catch an early direct flight to London. Throughout most of the flights I was lost in reverie, still mentally in Irian Jaya, in the jungles, on the mountains, with the Danis. I had gained so much. It had all been so worthwhile, the bad and the good were intertwined, both part of the learning and the teaching process. I couldn't have understood one without the other. Relaxing on the planes, whenever I drank tea I recollected what the English philosopher, Alan Watts, had so simplistically and accurately stated, 'You can never have the use of the inside of the cup without the outside. The inside and the outside go together, they are one'.

Each time I passed a check-in and luggage control the question of what was in my long, oddly-shaped package came up, but fortunately they were all prepared to listen patiently to my stories and finally allow me through. The fact that I had no luggage, was wearing a heavy mountain jacket and badly-torn rock climbing boots caked with mud and goodness knows what else, somehow convinced them that I was no threat to the airline. Just another eccentric Englishman who had possibly spent too much time in the jungles of Irian Jaya. The great news on returning to London was that I'd raised some substantial monies for the Red Cross and for two special children's charities.

Great Mountains Of The World

Everest *	8848 metres (29,028 ft)	Nepal
Aconcagua *	6560 metres (22,834 ft)	Argentina
McKinley *	6194 metres (20,320 ft)	Alaska
Kilimanjaro *	5895 metres (19,430 ft)	Tanzania
Elbrus *	5642 metres (18,510 ft)	Russia
Kenya	5199 metres (17,058 ft)	Kenya
Vinson Massif *	5140 metres (16,864 ft)	Antarctica
Carstensz Pyramid *	4884 metres (16,023 ft)	Indonesia
Ngga Pulu	4865 metres (15,960 ft)	Indonesia
Mont Blanc	4807 metres (15,771 ft)	France
Kosciusko	2228 metres (7,309 ft)	Australia

* The mountains comprising the Seven Summits; the highest mountain on each continent. (Until it became possible to access Irian Jaya, Kosciusko was treated as one of the seven mountains instead of Carstensz Pyramid).

It is however interesting to note that Hawaii's Mauna Kea mountain rises 5486 metres (18,000 ft) from the Pacific Ocean to the surface of the sea and above it there is then a further 4205 metres (13,796 ft). This combined total of 9691 metres (31,796 ft) is greater than Everest by 843 metres (2,768 ft).

Expedition Check List

CLOTHING AND EQUIPMENT

BODY WEAR
Thermal Underwear
Polar fleece jacket & pants
Rain jacket

Midwear (T-shirts etc)
Goretex jacket & pants
Casual clothing

HEAD WEAR
Balaclava
Sun hat
Snow and sun glasses

Woollen ski hat
Sun and lip creams

HAND WEAR
Finger gloves
Mittens and liners

Ski gloves
Gardening gloves (for razor rock climbing)

FOOT WEAR
Socks x 4 sets
Climbing boots

Trekking boots
Gaiters
Sandals

CAMPING GEAR AND SUNDRIES
Down sleeping bag
Thermorest
Toiletries and personal medication
Accessory items

Kit Bag
Personal first aid kit (To include anti-biotics and blister kit)
Plastic plate, cup and spoon
Foot powder

CLIMBING EQUIPMENT
Ice axe
Harness
Snap link carabiners
Ascenders
Water bottle
Climbing helmet

Crampons
Auto-locking carabiners
Figure of 8 descender
Headlamp with spare batteries
Climbing pack

IMPORTANT SUNDRIES
Camera, films
Knife
Compass
Umbrella

Dental gum, teeth floss
Plastic bags (Plenty)
Books, notepads
Airline face pads (Plenty)

Medical Recommendations

Polio	-	Within 10 years
Tetanus	-	Within 10 years
Typhoid Fever	-	Injections last 3 years, oral capsules require boosting annually.
Hepatitis A	-	Various injections to cover 1 month or several years.
Malaria Prevention	-	Weekly tablets to be taken one week before arrival in Indonesia and finish 4 weeks after departing. Daily tablets also to be taken one week before arrival and finish 4 weeks after departing.

People are mostly infected between dusk and dawn when the malaria-carrying mosquitos are usually biting. The incubation period before symptoms appear is commonly 12 to 30 days; depending on the species, the time can be sometimes even up to 10 months. Symptoms are variable but usually include fever, chills, and headache. The chances of contracting malaria are markedly reduced by taking certain preventive measures. They include the following:

1. Wear long-sleeved, light coloured clothing and long trousers, especially in the evening.
2. Use mosquito-proofed rooms or sleep in a bed with an insecticide impregnated mosquito net.
3. Apply an insect repellant to exposed skin.
4. Spray an insecticide containing pyrethrum indoors in the evening and at night.
5. Burn mosquito coils or use an electrical insecticide dispenser in the bedroom at night.
6. If possible, avoid going out between the hours of dusk and dawn when the mosquitos are most active.
7. Avoid dark coloured clothing as it attracts mosquitos, as may perfume, after-shave lotion, and cologne.
8. Avoid tight fitting clothing as mosquitos bite through it.

(One special tip, hopefully unnecessary: use toothpaste to soothe mosquito bites).

Glossary

abseil	Method of climbing down using double ropes (rappel).
arachnophobia	Fear of spiders.
guru	Spiritual teacher, guide; composed of indian words, gu meaning darkness or shadow ru meaning he who dispenses.
haiku	Japanese shortest forms of poetry in world literature. It evokes sabi, solitude, aloneness or detachment and wabi, the poignant spirit of poverty.
hishiryo	Thinking without effort, allowing your consciousness to expand naturally.
horim	Penis gourds worn by male Danis, also known as kotekas.
jeu	Dani hut
jumar	Metal clip used in climbing up to fasten a climber to a guide rope.
karma	Sanskrit word meaning action, positive or negative and the results of that action.
kinhin	The practice of zazen whilst carrying out an activity.
koan	Zen statement or riddle not immediately capable of being understood, sometimes paradoxical.
monsoon	Arabic word meaning a season of winds.
ophidophobia	Fear of snakes.
papisj	Dani word meaning the practice of wife swapping.
samurai	Japanese warrior (meaning those who serve).
satori	Enlightenment, awakening to the truth.
sensei	Japanese word meaning teacher.
shin	Spirit or mind.
sibs	Name of Dani clans.
sisu	Finnish word meaning to have determination and to never give in.
sumo	Japanese wrestling.
tai	Strength or force.
wasa	Technique or skill.
zazen	Concentrated practice of zen whilst sitting.
zen	Japanese philosophy practice used in meditation, a way of liberating the mind, reaching for enlightenment. (translated from the Chinese ch'an, in turn translated from the Sanskrit dhyana).